THE NARCISSIST'S PLAYBOOK

Other Books by the Author

Start Here: A Crash Course in Understanding, Navigating,
and Healing from Narcissistic Abuse

Out of the Fog: Moving from Confusion to Clarity
After Narcissistic Abuse

Insight Journal: A Three-Year Journal

The Five-Minute Gratitude Journal: A One-Year Journal

THE NARCISSIST'S PLAYBOOK

How to Identify, Disarm, and Protect Yourself from Narcissists, Sociopaths, Psychopaths, and Other Types of Manipulative and Abusive People

DANA MORNINGSTAR

Dedication

To everyone who is struggling to put the pieces of their life back together after a manipulative relationship. You are not alone, and you can do this.

A special thank you to Marisol, Agata, and my mother for all your feedback, insight, time, and support.

Disclaimer

This book is not intended to diagnose or treat anyone. Additionally, all names and examples have been changed to protect the identify of those involved. Any likeness to persons either living or dead is purely coincidental.

Table of Contents

PART 1

UNDERSTANDING MANIPULATION

INTRODUCTION

One of the most frequently-asked questions I get is how can it be possible that narcissists and other types of manipulative people, who have never met, can behave in almost the exact same way—sometimes down to saying the same things. While some are worse than others, they are still shades of the same color, leaving many survivors to wonder if they have some sort of playbook that guides their behavior.

The first two parts of this book cover everything having to do with manipulation that would be in a playbook if one existed. However, because understanding manipulation is only half the battle, the last two parts of this book cover how to break free from manipulation once and for all.

As you go through this book, you will most likely start to identify problematic behavior that many of the people in your life have. You may also become aware of some of your own problematic behaviors that you have developed, either as a way of coping with a dysfunctional relationship or as a result of a dysfunctional upbringing.

This can be concerning and can cause a person to wonder if they are manipulative, or if they are the problem.

Please don't panic and think you are a narcissist. Narcissism is a personality trait that we all have, and it exists on a continuum ranging from healthy to deadly. Healthy narcissism is when our level of self-orientation is such that we realize that we matter and are worth valuing and making a priority. We need to have a healthy level of narcissism if we are going to be able to set goals and be able to be self-protective. Narcissism only becomes problematic when a person's level of self-orientation is such that they are solely focused on themselves at the expense of, or to the destruction of, others.

If this book does its job, then it will bring to light a whole host of behaviors and personality traits that are problematic when taken to an extreme. The vast majority of people out there (myself included) have or had some of these traits. This is normal and is the result of growing up in a dysfunctional home or society, which we all do. If you are introspective, odds are you will see some of these traits within yourself. These traits don't make you bad, wrong, or somehow to blame. Being manipulated or abused is never your fault. Most of the time we've developed these traits as a way to cope, and I hope that by the end of this book you'll be able to see human behavior—others as well as your own with a level of clarity you need in order to move forward and heal.

CHAPTER 1

WE ALL THINK WE CAN SPOT A PROBLEM FOR WHAT IT IS

We all think we'd be able to see a problematic situation for what it is, and be able to get out of harm's way. *And most of the time we would be wrong.* I recently came across a video that was tragic because of the magnitude of the situation, and upsetting because of the comments that were made. The video was of two tourists filming their afternoon on a beach in Thailand. While they were recording, the ocean began to recede. Moments later, numerous boats that had been docked in several feet of water, were now left teetering on wet sand. With this realization, the tourists' laughter and good times were quickly replaced by confusion and chaos.

The camera panned around to capture this strange new shoreline. Dozens of confused tourists just like them stared into the sandy distance, trying to make sense of what was happening. Their stunned silence was soon replaced with attempts to make sense of what was happening. One tourist asked another if perhaps the receding water could have something to do with the earthquake that happened earlier that day. The other tourist didn't think it was related.

Their conversation was cut short by a loud commotion off in the distance. The camera then panned to dozens of panicked locals running as fast as they could away from the beach. Confused by what the locals knew that they didn't, the tourists turned the camera back towards the ocean. This time there was more to see than hundreds of feet of wet sand; there was a strange-looking wave off in the distance. Still uncertain about what was going on, but knowing that if the locals were running they probably should too, the tourists joined in the mad dash away from the shore.

Within minutes, a tsunami decimated the shores of 12 countries along the Indian Ocean, killing over 230,000 people. What started out as a vacation video ended up being some of the only footage of this tragic event. When the video ended, I scrolled down to read the comments and was both surprised and horrified by all the victim blaming and shaming. I found it insensitive, disturbing, and bizarre that anyone would think that those who died in the tsunami were somehow at fault.

As I continued to read through these unsettling comments, I noticed that there were three main themes:

1. The victims should have known this was a tsunami.
2. The victims should have been running away and were dumb for just standing around.

3. That nothing like this would ever happen to the commenters because they would have known better and gotten out of harm's way.

I was stunned by the parallels between the victims of a tsunami and the targets of manipulation, as well as those who blame both for having their lives destroyed.

In both a literal tsunami and an emotional tsunami that is the result of extreme manipulation, there is no shortage of people who play the part of the Monday-morning quarterback. It's easy to know what to do when you have the emotional distance of not being involved and the benefit of knowing how everything will play out. It's significantly more difficult to navigate a stressful situation when you are in it.

Let's back up for a moment and examine what happened here. So why didn't the couple on the beach run? Why did they just stand there as the water left the shore? Why didn't the tourists realize that the growing wave off in the distance was a tsunami?

Simply put, the couple didn't run because they didn't think they were in danger.

Like most of us, I'm sure they had heard of a tsunami. But also like most of us, they weren't familiar with the early warning signs of one. After all, I'd imagine that when most people think of a tsunami they visualize a towering wall of water, not the shoreline receding. So, because they weren't familiar with the early warning signs, and because the tsunami that they were experiencing didn't match the image in their mind, they didn't see it for what it was until it was too late.

If identifying something as large as a tsunami is difficult, then think about how challenging it can be to identify something more subtle, such as manipulation. And much like with the tsunami, our biggest chance at escaping devastating consequences is to learn about the early warning signs, so we know what manipulation *really* looks like.

CHAPTER 2

WHY WE TEND TO THINK BAD THINGS WON'T HAPPEN TO US

While I was in the process of writing this book, I had a conversation with a woman who worked at a domestic violence shelter. She was venting her frustrations about how victims of natural disasters aren't blamed for having their lives destroyed, but victims of manipulation or other forms of abuse are. I told her that I used to think this was the case as well...until I saw the video about the tsunami.

Many people might think that there is a difference between being caught in a tsunami and staying in a relationship with a manipulative person--that the person who stays in a manipulative relationship is choosing to be there. And if they don't like how they are being treated, then they should leave. While that may be logical, it's overly simplistic. No one consciously chooses to be manipulated, just like no one consciously chooses to be in a tsunami. In both cases, people get *trapped* in these situations because they don't understand what's happening early on, and by the time they do, the stress, fear, and overwhelming feelings of how to escape can be debilitating.

Because manipulation is confusing for everyone except the manipulator, those on the receiving end of it as well as those around them tend to misunderstand what's happening. For these reasons, manipulation is often denied or minimized, and is not seen as the damaging force that it is. It's been my experience that many, if not most, people view an abusive relationship as one where there is physical violence taking place. And if the target of this abuse leaves or if the physical abuse stops and instead switches to verbal and emotional, then the relationship is no longer considered abusive. Make no mistake: a manipulative relationship is an abusive relationship, and an abusive relationship is a manipulative one as well. Abuse and manipulation go hand-in-hand. This is why it's so difficult for a person to get and stay out of a relationship like this.

If the target is fortunate enough to get out of a relationship like this, they don't often feel that way. Instead, they may feel profoundly broken and overwhelmed with how to move forward. And blaming them for what happened isn't helpful; it's re-victimizing. On the opposite end of the spectrum is continually reminding them of how lucky they are that things weren't worse isn't helpful either. If anything, it can come across as invalidating, as the target may feel bad for not being able to focus on the positive. It's like telling a victim of a burglary that they are lucky they weren't killed. While this is true, it doesn't mean that what they experienced wasn't traumatic, and glossing over it and focusing on the bright side when they are in pain is insensitive.

Additionally, even though the relationship is over, it doesn't mean the manipulation or abuse has stopped. It often hasn't. Sometimes the abuse just takes on a different form. If the former target has children with this person, then they will most likely be on the receiving end of all kinds of abusive phone calls and text messages, not to mention frivolous lawsuits, wildly untrue allegations, and stalking. So trying to "get over" a trauma like this when the trauma is still occurring is impossible.

That would never happen to me

When we see people in any sort of problematic situation, whether it be a tsunami or an abusive relationship, it can be easy to think we would handle the situation differently. Thinking that these kinds of traumas only happen to other people, is, ironically, part of the reason we get tangled up in these situations to begin with. There are four thoughts we all tend to have when it comes to traumatic people or events:

1. We don't think *really* bad things could or would happen to us.
2. We think we'd be able to identify any danger for what it is and be able to move out of harm's way.
3. We think that if we did get caught up in some sort of problematic situation we'd handle it appropriately.
4. We think that if we've experienced a problematic situation once that it would never happen again.

For the sake of clarity, let's go through each of these points in more detail.

1. We don't think *really* bad things could or would happen to us.

On some level we know that bad things could happen to us. It's why we take precautions such as wearing our seatbelt, locking our doors, and buying insurance. However, I think most of us do these things more for peace of mind than we do because we fully comprehend what all is possible.

Until we experience any type of crisis, we don't tend to think it will happen to us. Because we may only see stories of crisis on the news, it can be easy to think that these kinds of things couldn't happen to us. This is known "irrational invincibility." We live in a mild state of denial about what could happen to us is, in part, because we need to feel safe in order to function. If we fully realized that all sorts of bad things could happen to us too, then we might experience such chronic anxiety that we wouldn't be able to get out of bed or leave the house. And so, we tell ourselves that we have nothing to worry about, because we are somehow smarter, more observant, or better equipped than *those* people. It's especially easy to fall into this thinking, if we've never been in a traumatic situation.

Even if we have had something traumatic happen, oftentimes we tend to see it as a fluke and something that would never happen again—or if it did happen again, that we'd see it coming. However, because every problematic person and situation comes across in a different way, this is rarely the case.

12

2. We think we'd be able to identify any problem for what it is and be able to move out of harm's way.

We all struggle with identifying certain problematic situations for what they are. It can be even more difficult for us to identify what's going on in time for us to get out of harm's way. Just like with the tsunami, we all think we know what an abusive person or manipulation looks like. And again, most of the time we would be wrong. Problematic situations rarely come across as problematic—at least at first, and they definitely don't come across like we imagine they will. And, to add to the challenge, these problems usually won't happen in the same way next time. This is especially the case with manipulation and abuse.

Manipulative or abusive people don't always look like they could be manipulative or abusive, and they don't always mistreat everyone they are around. Sometimes they can be friendly, funny, caring, and attractive. They can be male or female, young or old, any nationality, religion, or sexual orientation, and work in any profession.

The only way to have a chance at keeping ourselves safe in any kind of situation, especially from manipulative people, is to take protective action when we spot some red flags. The challenge with this is that red flags aren't seen, *they are felt*, and the early warning signs we do get *are only signs*—they aren't concrete proof of a problem. If we have concrete proof that we are in danger, it's generally too late.

When we don't have concrete proof that there is a problem, taking any sort of action can feel like we are overreacting. This is especially the case if we take action and then it turns out that whatever we were concerned about doesn't happen and everything turns out okay. When this is the case, we can feel embarrassed *and mistakenly learn the lesson that we were wrong to act.* Erring on the side of caution is all any of us can do, and in terms of safety, it's always the right thing to do.

For example, we see a story on the news of a woman who was attacked in a parking lot. She tells the reporter that she heard someone walking quickly behind her, but didn't run or grab her mace because she assumed he was in a hurry. Because we know how her situation turned out, it's easy for us to play the role of Monday-morning quarterback and criticize her decision not to act, because we know the outcome.

When a situation like this is unfolding, taking action such as grabbing the mace on our key chain, taking a sharp turn in another direction, calling the police, or even simply walking faster can feel like we are over-reacting because we don't know *for sure* if we are in danger. And taking preventive action like this can cause us to feel hyper-vigilant, rude, or foolish if the person behind us isn't a criminal but someone who is simply walking fast.

Hearing someone walking fast behind us is one of the more concrete early warning signs that we may have, as most are significantly more subtle, especially when it comes to manipulation. And here's the thing: all early-warning signs, no matter how obvious, can be easily rationalized and glossed over. So just because we can offer up an explanation, it doesn't mean we are right, and it doesn't mean that what we are experiencing isn't a problem.

The only way we can tell if we took the right action is if we are able to avoid harm. The challenge with this is that we will never know if our action saved us from harm or if it was a false alarm from the beginning. The reality is that the only way for us to truly find out if we were, in fact, in harm's way is to actually get hurt. Obviously, this is not a good plan, and yet, this is what so many of us have done—myself included. Waiting until we are absolutely certain that there is a problem before we take action, is waiting too long. In order for us to avoid potential harm, we have to become okay with taking protective action, even if it turns out it's a false alarm.

To do this, we need to do four things:

- **Realize that taking protective action when something feels off isn't being over-reactive.**

   When we get that funny feeling that something is "off," it's important we listen. More often than not, that feeling is right. Moving yourself out of potential harm's way is not being over-reactive.

- **Realize that taking action, even if the danger turns out to be a false alarm, doesn't mean that taking protective action was a mistake or an over-reaction.**

   If we are able to take action early enough, we will have avoided harm. In terms of personal safety, we will rarely know if what we experienced was a false alarm or if we did, in fact, avoid danger. In terms of relationships, I know that many survivors of abuse struggle with their perception of events. They fear that they are misreading a person or situation due to feeling hyper-vigilant and distrusting. They often want concrete proof that this person is indeed problematic before they leave, as they fear they might be walking away from a great person. A situation, especially a relationship, isn't worth being in if it's costing you your safety or sanity. Hopefully, by the end of this book you'll have more clarity about why certain things feel off so that you won't need others to validate your decisions, and, instead, can find that validation from within.

- **Get comfortable with taking protective action even if things turn out to be a false alarm.**

    There will always be people in your life who don't agree with the choices you make. Don't wait for everyone to agree that you are doing the right thing before you protect yourself. The more you practice making decisions and not needing the approval of others, the more empowered you will be.

- **Get comfortable with other people not agreeing with your decisions.**

    I commonly hear from people who are planning to leave an abusive relationship that they are getting pressure from others, and that it's rude for them to not tell their abusive spouse they are leaving ahead of time, or that it's rude for them to go no contact with hurtful people. You need to do what you need to do. So what if other people think you are overly cautious or rude when it comes to how you protect yourself? They aren't the ones who have to live with the consequences; you do. And, ironically, if something bad does happen, they'll be some of the first people that will ask you why you didn't get out of harm's way sooner.

Additionally, even if we are able to identify the early signs for what they are, when we are under extreme or sudden stress, our physiological defenses of fight, flight, or freeze are triggered. Our freeze defense is usually deployed first, causing us to feel like we are knocked off balance, leaving us frozen in stunned silence. These different defenses happen below our conscious awareness, and we don't choose which ones we use—*our brain chooses for us.*

3. We think that if we did get caught up in some sort of problematic situation, we'd handle it appropriately.

We've all heard stories on the news of people running back into a burning house to try to save their photo albums, or who have a violent ex that they decide to meet in an isolated place, only to be seriously hurt or killed. We might wonder what on Earth were they thinking?

When we hear of people acting in ways that seem nonsensical, it can be easy to think that we would never act that way—that we would handle things differently. In addition to having the knowledge of how their situation played out, we also have the benefit of being able to think clearly because we aren't involved in their situation. When we experience something out of the ordinary, regardless of whether or not it's stressful, it knocks us off balance, and when this happens, we aren't thinking clearly and default into doing what we routinely do.

For example, in his book *The Gift of Fear*, author Gavin de Becker writes about a study done on people who had received mail bombs. He said that if a person gets a suspicious package in the mail, they do two things: *they joke about how the package looks like a mail bomb, and then they open it.* Why would someone do this? Simply put, they weren't expecting to ever be sent a mail bomb. Since they didn't want to over-react or look foolish for calling the police, they tell themselves it's probably just a strange package and nothing to worry about.

What's even more interesting (and more useful) is to know that while our brains are having a delay in processing what's going on, that on another, deeper level we are aware that we are in danger. A way we can tell is if we (or someone else around us who is experiencing the same event such standing next to someone who receives a mail bomb) is feeling confused, and then clearly states the obvious, or begins using sarcasm or dark humor to describe what's going on. We unconsciously use dark humor as a way to relieve our anxiety about a stressful situation.

What's happening here is that the danger is registering on one level but being suppressed on another. This is why erring on the side of caution is so important. If you are feeling confused, fearful, or have concerns something or someone might be dangerous or deadly, this is not normal. If you are still in doubt, it can help to remind yourself that you don't normally feel this way around most people or in most situations.

When we encounter anything that we struggle to acknowledge, such as our boss being inappropriate or our partner having squirrelly behavior, we attempt to make sense of what's going on, because this feels like the logical thing to do. However, if we are hoping that what we are experiencing isn't the problem we know deep down that it is, we will cling to any rationalization we can come up with and tell ourselves that it's no big deal. For example, we may tell ourselves that our boss is being flirty because he's from another country and that's just his culture, or because he's older or younger and that's just how men at that age act, or that he's just a flirt with everyone so that makes it okay. Or for our partner, we may tell ourselves that he's stressed or busy and that's why they aren't returning our texts, or we may believe them when they say that all these flirty texts they keep getting are from exes who won't leave them alone (but, of course, that doesn't explain why they continued to respond back).

If we are knocked off balance by an event that causes both confusion and sudden or extreme stress, we will go into fight, flight, or freeze mode. For example, after the mail bomb explodes, everyone in the office will most likely either stand there in shock or they will begin to panic--pushing and climbing over each other in order to get out of the building, or doing nonsensical things such as trying to get back to their office so they can get their briefcase while the building is on fire. Or, a boss makes a sexual advance and we freeze, not able to know what to say or what to do as he gropes us. And after the event is over we feel guilty, gross, confused, and upset for just standing there and not doing anything to stop it.

The idea of running back to our office to get our briefcase, standing there while we are being groped, or running back into a burning house to get photos might sound absurd, but it's not. It's what happens when the critical thinking part of our brain goes off line and the more primitive parts of our brain that control our flight, flight, or freeze defenses take over. The result is that instead of being able to be responsive, we become reactive. This is why we do not act logically, or "like ourselves" when we are under extreme stress. In order to help you to shift from being reactive to being responsive, several strategies are mentioned in part four of this book.

4. We think that if we've experienced a problematic situation once that it would never happen again.

In terms of abuse and manipulation, we may think that we'll never get caught up in it again. However, from my own experience, as well as hearing about the experiences of tens of thousands of others, this is not true. What I have seen and personally experienced is that if a person gets caught up with a manipulative or abusive person once, the odds of it happening again *increase, not decrease.*

There are two main reasons for this: 1. That they think they know all of the signs and what to avoid next time around, or 2. They may think that this problematic person was a narcissist, sociopath, or psychopath, and because less than five percent of the population has these personality disorders that must mean that what happened to them was a fluke—along the lines of getting struck by lightning. And because it was a fluke, they aren't on the lookout for signs of what to avoid next time, because they don't think there will be a next time.

The reality is that every manipulative person comes across differently. Some are charming and great listeners, and some are insufferable and self-absorbed. They might be someone we date, or they might be someone we know from work—or even someone we consider a friend. They can work in any profession, be any age, gender, sexual orientation, nationality, religion, astrological sign, you name it. So it's important that we aren't linking up the incorrect cause and effect and thinking that men, spiritual leaders, redheads, or Scorpios are the problem. It's manipulative behavior that's the problem, and it's more common than most people realize.

CHAPTER 3

SEEING MANIPULATION
AS IT'S HAPPENING

Seeing manipulation for what it is, while it's occurring, is a process best described as an evolution of awakening. As you get clarity about what manipulation is, the behaviors involved, and how it happens, the more adept you will be at seeing it for what it is. This awareness happens in phases, and each phase comes with its own set of challenges.

Phase One: Awareness of Manipulation after the Fact.

Phase one happens with hindsight--potentially months, years, or even decades after the "manipulationship" has ended. We might have gone into therapy because we were anxious, angry, or depressed but didn't know why, and then came to learn that it's because we had been manipulated and abused, or we might have realized the truth after they ran off with our life savings, the promotion they kept promising never comes, or their affairs began to surface.

This first phase of awareness often brings validation as we start to realize that we feel angry, victimized, and used for a reason. Soon after we are able to acknowledge what really happened, anger settles in. We most likely feel angry at the manipulator for all the damage they did to us. We may also be angry at ourselves for not seeing the manipulation when it was happening.

The challenge with this phase is to see manipulative behavior as the problem. It's understandable to think that the manipulator was the problem, and if they are gone then so is the problem. However, while that specific person may have been the biggest manipulator you've ever come across, odds are they weren't the first, and they won't be the last. In short, it's important that we see that manipulative behavior is the problem, and that this behavior isn't limited to the person who hurt you.

Phase Two: Awareness of Manipulation While It's Happening.

With phase one, we were only able to see manipulation after the fact. With phase two, we are now better able to see manipulation while it's occurring. This phase of awareness is best achieved if time has been spent learning the variety of ways manipulation can and does happen. The more aware you are of this behavior the less you will be confused by it, leaving you better equipped to respond to it effectively. Simply having the understanding and validation of what behaviors are manipulative can be enough to set a person free from it and start them on the path to healing.

The challenge with this phase is with being able to validate ourselves. While we may be more aware of problematic behavior as it's occurring, we may also struggle with doubting our perception of events, and fearing that we are hyper-vigilant, and misreading the situation due to our previous experience with manipulators. This self-doubt can cause us to look to others for validation. The problem is that unless those other people are deeply familiar with manipulation, the odds that they'll be able to spot it are slim to none. Instead, what tends to happen is that they offer up excuses and alternate explanations for what you are experiencing. This creates more confusion and doubt. Fearing that we are over-reacting, we give the manipulator the benefit of the doubt...which only keeps us stuck in a bad situation that much longer. You need to be able to determine if something is a problem for you, and not continually ask others. *Because as long as you need validation from others, your life is not your own.*

Phase Three: Developing a Planned Response to Manipulative Behavior.

Phase three involves developing the skills to be able to prepare for, respond to, and effectively disable manipulation while it's happening. The most powerful skills needed for phase three are: learning how to set boundaries, refining your situational awareness, and being proactive in your approach. This book, especially parts four and five, will help you to do just that. These skills are significantly easier once you have a solid grasp on seeing manipulative behavior for what it is and learning to validate yourself--the skills found in phases one and two.

What's important right now is to understand that there are different phases of awareness and how they happen. The reason this understanding is so important is because seeing behavior clearly is a process; it's not an event. And it's a process that will take practice, self-reflection, patience, and self-compassion as you go through it.

The skills needed in phase three are some of the most difficult, as they will require:

- Identifying what behavior tends to knock you off balance
- Identifying your normal responses when this happens
- Learning some new skills to do instead
- Examining what worked and what didn't
- Continually practicing and giving yourself compassion and grace while you are learning

There are four main challenges with this phase:

1. To hold your boundaries with the manipulator whose behavior will continue to knock you off balance.
2. To remain in control of your interactions with the manipulator as best as you can.
3. To not let the well-intended bad advice or pressure from others knock you off course.
4. To not be so hard on yourself when you don't do things exactly like you wanted to, and to keep any feelings of

frustration, overwhelm, or low self-esteem in check so they don't derail your progress.

CHAPTER 4

WHAT MANIPULATION IS AND ISN'T

What Manipulation Is

In terms of personal relationships, manipulation is a slow and steady imbalance of power. This imbalance is created when one person leverages the emotions of fear, obligation, or guilt against another with the ultimate goal of getting their way. This can create an almost seemingly unbearable tension, as the direct or implied threat of some sort of punishment hangs in the balance. Once this imbalance takes place, the relationship ceases to be healthy (if it ever was), and stagnates. At this point forward, the target is on edge around this person, waiting for the next inappropriate request or radical change in temperament to occur. Any of the target's attempts at authentic connection or communication become silenced, and are replaced with resentment, insecurity, and fear. And much like a spinning top that gets knocked off center, as long as manipulation is present, the relationship will wobble until it topples over.

While it can come across in a wide variety of ways, the common denominator tends to be either a boundary push, such as an inappropriate or uncomfortable request, or a flat-out deception. Manipulation, no matter how mild, is progressive, and grows with every subsequent boundary push. However, the target is often unaware that these subtle violations are happening and that the dynamic has become increasingly more imbalanced and one-sided. (Boundary pushes and other helpful terminology are covered in Chapter 8.)

The Spectrum of Manipulation

Manipulation ranges from mild to malicious, direct to indirect, verbal to nonverbal, unintentional to intentional, and annoying to deadly. Anywhere along the spectrum is a problem.

On the milder and annoying end of the manipulation spectrum is the parent who tries to guilt their adult child into calling or visiting more. It's the boss who subtly pushes us into working harder, longer, and faster in order to get that promotion that never comes. It's the significant other who is enjoyable to be around—as long as they get their way. It's the friend who becomes difficult, snarky, cold, or punishing if you have something positive in your life that they don't.

On the more extreme end is when the attempt is made to hold you emotionally hostage. The stakes at this level are high, and the intention is clear: either do what the manipulator wants or they will hurt themselves, be hurt by someone else, or will hurt you or those you love. The pressure to act can feel unbearable, as a person often feels they have no choice but to do what seems safest--which often means giving in to the emotional terrorist's demand. The catch is that there is usually no end to the pressure from a manipulator. Giving in doesn't make things better in the long run; it only relieves the target's stress and the threat of the situation in the short term. Unfortunately, giving in to this kind of behavior doesn't mean that everything is now fine; it means that this dynamic has hit a new low and that the manipulator will attempt to hold you hostage the next time they want something.

Some examples of someone trying to hold you emotionally hostage are:

- Threatening suicide if you don't reopen communication.
- Threatening to start drinking, using drugs, or other forms of self-harm if you don't reopen contact with them.
- Threatening to file for full custody, withhold visitation, withhold their visits to the children, not pay child support, or to make the target and the children homeless if they don't get their way.
- Threatening to release sexy, nude, or otherwise personal photos or emails of you online or to friends, family, and coworkers.
- Threatening to ruin your career if you don't have sex with them, lie for them, or otherwise do what they want.

Having a manipulative person in your life is an anxiety-inducing, emotionally, and sometimes physically unsafe way to live. Trying to get better at meeting their demands, attempting to cope with the extreme stress, or hoping that the manipulator will change aren't good long-term strategies.

At its most severe, manipulation is a power play that's rooted in a dangerous degree of entitlement or sadism. The driving force at this level is a pathological need for control. The only way this type of manipulator is satisfied is if the target is sufficiently destroyed emotionally or physically—or both.

At this degree, it's common for the target's reality to have been replaced with the manipulator's, and they may feel they are to blame for any abuse that is occurring. They no longer have a solid sense of self, and their actions are primarily fueled by fear of what the manipulator will do if they don't comply, fear of losing the relationship, or fear of living without them. When people experience this degree of extreme stress and resulting mental anguish—especially at the hands of someone they care about, they can feel like they are losing their mind. This is especially the case if they are unaware that they are being manipulated or abused. If they realize they are being mistreated, they may feel profoundly confused and upset that they could love or miss a person who treats them so terribly. If they don't realize they are being mistreated, and instead think of their relationship as having "issues" then they tend to feel emotionally devastated or broken but not know why. This confusion, more often than not, will cause the target to continually support or defend the manipulator, claiming that they love them. This isn't love. Love doesn't hurt; it's the lack of love that hurts.

What Manipulation Isn't

While it's important to understand what manipulation is, it's also important to understand what manipulation *isn't*. Manipulation isn't a personality conflict, a matter of perception, miscommunication, influence, the result of karma, bad luck, or something you attracted. Each of these five points are worth addressing so you don't get derailed by this thinking.

1. Manipulation is not a personality (or zodiac sign) conflict. Zodiac signs or personality conflicts are often blamed when tension and difficulty arise. However, if more attempts at communication only seem to make things worse, then there is more going on. This is especially the case if the dynamic started out great and then suddenly goes off the rails and you have no idea why. If this is a continual pattern, it can help to think about what might have led up to this erratic and anxiety-inducing behavior, because you may be locked in a power play and not even realize it.

2. Manipulation is not a matter of perception. Facts and perception are different, but are often mistaken for the same thing. Manipulation, just like verbal bullying or physical abuse, isn't a matter of perception. There are behaviors a person can point to in order to show that they are being targeted. However, pinpointing this behavior and having others see it for what it is can be difficult due to lack of knowledge or real-world experience with major forms of manipulation. Most people, even many mental health professionals, aren't able to see manipulation and abuse for what it is.

When manipulation is subtle, such as a snide comment or small changes in the manipulator's behavior that create a tense environment, such as threatening looks or an icy presence, these behaviors can be difficult for others to see. This is because they are only seeing snippets of this kind of behavior and because they aren't on the receiving end of this, they are lacking context. However, no matter how severe and obvious manipulation may be, there will still be those who can't or won't see it for what it is—which will be covered later in this book. For the target, having their experience denied, minimized, or invalidated can make them question their sanity and wonder if they are making a big deal out of nothing; it can also feel infuriating and re-victimizing—because it is.

Some examples of subtle manipulative behavior are:

- A passive-aggressive boss who continues to change your schedule, and either doesn't tell you or tells you at the last minute—and then gets upset with you for showing up late or not showing up at all.

- A coworker who went from being an office friend to a standoffish stranger once you got something they wanted, such as a promotion, a new car, a new relationship, a client complementing you and not them, and so on. Things seemed fine on Friday but, come Monday, there is now an icy divide, and they've become difficult, rude, or demanding.

- An ex-boyfriend who threatens to commit suicide if you don't call him back.

- A significant other gives you the silent treatment after you disagree with them.

- A parent who tells you that if you don't take over the family business they will disown you.

If this kind of manipulation is more on the mild end, such as a co-worker being difficult, their behavior may be confusing if they have some legitimate issues with your work performance. It's okay for someone to have an issue with you or your work, but it's not okay for them to create a hostile environment, plant seeds of insecurity, become hyper-critical, impossible to please, or threatening. Just like it's okay for someone to be frustrated or angry, but it's not okay for them to become abusive in any way *because* they were frustrated or angry. For example, people with abusive behavior will often say that they yelled at or hit their target because their target upset them. However, just because they are upset, doesn't mean that it's okay to yell at or hit someone. They can be upset and then go for a walk, leave the room, vent to a friend, journal, get in their car and turn on loud music or scream, you name it. It's not expecting too much for others to treat you with respect; it's the basics of adult behavior.

3. Manipulation is not miscommunication. Sincere miscommunication can easily be cleared up with an assertive, solutions-oriented, and relatively *brief* conversation. If the conversation continually gets dragged off course with blame shifting, deflection, projection, triangulation, or behavior that shows anything other than a sincere desire to be accountable and work towards a solution, then the issue isn't with communication. All of these behaviors and many others are covered more in-depth in Chapter Eight.

The reason issues don't get resolved with manipulators is simple: they don't want them to get resolved. They want to get their way, or, they may feel smug and superior by being able to create so much drama.

If confronted, the manipulator may exclaim that the target is paranoid and has misunderstood their actions. The manipulator may even act deeply hurt by the accusations and be shocked that you would ever think that they would be manipulative or hurtful. If the manipulator is emotionally immature, then they might not realize they are being manipulative because they lack the self-awareness to see that their behavior is a problem. However, the more intentional and malicious manipulators out there know exactly what they are doing. If you find yourself explaining the basics of adult behavior to a fully-functioning adult, such as why it's not okay to flirt, lie, cheat, steal, hit, and so on, then this is a problem, and they are most likely playing dumb in order to avoid consequences. Regardless of how unaware they previously were of their behavior, if you've let them know they've crossed a line, then now they know, and there is no more excuse. If they continue to cross the line in the future, then you know it's intentional.

What tends to be the case with people who have such deeply dysfunctional behavior is that it's rarely limited to the one or two issues you have with them. They have problematic behavior across the board. What this will mean to you is that you will have to continually draw and hold the line. As soon as one issue gets resolved, another one pops up, and this is exhausting. If the manipulator continues to see no issue with their behavior, what commonly happens is they start accusing the target of being difficult or hyper-sensitive. This can cause the target to start questioning themselves and their expectations--and to stop bringing issues up in an attempt to keep the peace. The result is that the target becomes passive and submissive as they begin to stifle their thoughts, feelings, and opinions.

The target on the receiving end of this crazy-making behavior is often left feeling angry, frustrated, irritated, confused, and resentful at why getting answers from the other person is so difficult. This may be especially confusing if the target thinks they already know the worst of the worst: the manipulator stole from them, their children, or their business, got someone pregnant, racked up debt they didn't know about, and so on. Because of this, the target might be confused as to why they are still not owning up to everything—after all, they already know what they did.

If you still have to drag the full truth out of someone, or if they are still hiding details, it's generally because what you know is the tip of the iceberg.

The only other viable explanation is that they are trying to win some power struggle that exists in their mind. Regardless of their intention; either way you look at it, you lose.

If they truly don't know how hurtful they are being, then an open and honest dialog should result in changed behavior on their end. If the only changed behavior you see is them changing up their game, then they aren't sorry and their behavior will continue. At this point, the only solution is getting distance from them. Keep in mind that while manipulation isn't miscommunication, it is a form of *indirect* communication. Their actions are telling you everything that you need to know.

The Differences between Solutions-Oriented Communication and Controlling Communication

The intentions behind communication falls into one of two main categories: solutions-oriented and controlling.

If a person genuinely wants to resolve a conflict, they will:

- Talk openly about the issues and concerns they have with you.
- Seek to hear your viewpoint and your feelings.
- Seek to explore the divide between your perspective, feelings, wants, and needs, and their own.
- Sincerely accept responsibility for their actions.
- Work toward a solution.

If someone is trying to control you, they will:

- Shut down communication about issues and concerns that you have with them.

- Spin the conversation around to focus on every problem that they have with you, or point out everything they've done for you.

- Minimize your viewpoint and feelings.

- Invalidate your feelings, and insist that they are right.

- Try and make you feel guilty, bad, stupid, or crazy for having any issue or concern.

- Avoid taking any sincere responsibility (they will justify, argue, defend, blame, deny, or minimize their behavior).

- Refuse to be totally open about their actions, and will only admit to what you already know.

4. Manipulation is not the same as positive influence. Sometimes manipulation is confused for positive influence, as both involve leveraging another person's emotions. A good coach, mentor, parent, or friend often use influence. However, there are five main differences regarding intention, encouragement, persuasion, the intended result, the actual result, and who benefits. In order for behavior to be considered a positive influence, *all five* of these criteria have to benefit the other person. However, in order for behavior to be considered manipulative (or problematic at best), *only one* of the criteria has to benefit the manipulator.

Intention.

With manipulation, the intention is for the manipulator *to get* their way or some desired result. With influence, the intention is *to encourage* (not get) another to do something that's in their best interest.

Persuasion and Encouragement.

With manipulation, pressure is used to gain control, and the person on the receiving end of this is unable to disagree without some sort of conflict or consequence.

With influence, pressure is not used to control the other person; instead, persuasion is used to encourage the other person. The person being influenced is able to decline the persuasion without fear or concern of being punished.

The intended result.

With manipulation, the goal is for the manipulator to get their way.

With influence, the goal is for the other person to be encouraged to something in their best interest. Whether they take action is up to them, and it is not a part of the intended result.

The actual result.

With manipulation, the manipulator gets their way through the use of pressure and control. As a result, tension and resentment begin to grow, and the relationship feels unbalanced and emotionally unsafe.

With influence, the influencer isn't trying to get their way; they are only trying to encourage another. As a result, trust and connection grow, and the relationship feels strengthened and emotionally safe.

Who benefits.

With manipulation, the manipulator is the one who benefits.

With influence, the person being influenced is the one who benefits.

When Good Intentions Go Wrong

Sometimes good intentions can unintentionally become manipulative, controlling, or problematic and result in disastrous outcomes. For this reason, it's important that we are continually checking in to make sure that the actual result matches our intention. This can be done by taking those five criteria listed above and turning them into questions that we periodically ask ourselves. These five questions are:

- What is my intention?
- Am I using persuasion and encouragement or pressure and control?
- What is the result I'm after?
- What is the result I'm getting?
- Who benefits from this result?

After answering these questions, you'll be better able to see any adjustments that need to be made in order to keep positive intentions and influence in alignment with positive results.

5. Manipulation is not karma, bad luck, or something you attracted.

When we are continually on the receiving end of manipulation, and feel powerless at stopping it, we can start to wonder why we are a lightning rod for such mistreatment. In an attempt to figure out why we keep attracting problematic people, we may start to wonder if we have some negative karma to work off or are being punished by God. In this search for answers, many wind up coming across The Law of Attraction.

If you are unfamiliar with The Law of Attraction, it's the belief that like energy attracts like energy. And since everything in the universe is made up of energy, including us, we are able to control what we attract by changing our energy. Simply put, good energy attracts good things, and bad energy attracts bad things. However, this is not always how life works. Sometimes bad things happen to good people and good things happen to bad people. So while The Law of Attraction may seem to work some of the time doesn't mean that it works. After all, a broken clock is right twice a day.

When we think we are able to influence events outside of our control, we are engaging in what's known as "magical thinking." The reason this thinking is called "magical" is because our actions aren't impacting the outcome—even though on the surface they may appear to be.

Here is an example of what I commonly see: A person is scared or tired of attracting hurtful people. And because there are things going on outside of their awareness (such as not knowing when they are being mistreated, how their vulnerabilities are being exploited, or when they are being manipulated), it can feel like there are outside forces at work. They begin reading about The Law of Attraction, and start setting their intention to attract good, solid people into their life. Inevitably, some charming, attractive, seemingly like-minded person shows up. In their mind, they think they attracted this person into their life, and since good energy only attracts good energy, they aren't going to use a healthy level of discernment or boundaries because they don't think they need to. If any red flags surface, they are quick to justify them, as they don't want any doubt or negative thoughts to lower their energy. The result is that these relationships can go from a romantic whirlwind to an emotionally devastating tornado once they realize their perfect partner isn't at all what they thought.

There is significantly more involved to understanding the psychological principles behind The Law of Attraction that make it seem like it works, and why it's dangerous. However, because a more in-depth look is outside the scope of this book, I have a series of videos on my website where I warmly welcome any conversation on this topic. If you are interested, please visit:

www.thriveafterabuse.com/lawofattraction

CHAPTER 5

WHO CAN BE MANIPULATED AND WHO CAN BE MANIPULATIVE

Who Can Be Manipulated

Manipulation can happen anywhere, by anyone, to anyone. It can happen between friends, family, coworkers, church acquaintances, neighbors, or strangers. It exists between people of any gender, age, religion, profession, sexual orientation, nationality, or education level. Manipulation can be malicious or mild, and can be intentional or unintentional. It can come from a predator or from a well-intended person with unreasonable expectations and dysfunctional ways of getting their needs met.

There is a misconception out there that those who are involved with manipulators do so because they've experienced abuse or neglect as a child. This isn't always the case, *and even it was, healing these wounds is not the full solution.* This line of thinking can cause a person to spend years in therapy examining every painful childhood event, while not addressing other contributing factors. However, by the time you get to the end of this book, these other factors will be much more clear.

Additionally, not all manipulators are malicious or intentional. Some people with codependent behavior may be well-intended, but in ways that are controlling or manipulative. They may have an excessive focus on taking care of or trying to get others to change—regardless if their help is wanted. This type of behavior often exhausts them and breeds hostility and resentment in those they are trying to change or help. Because this manipulative behavior is not malicious or intentional, it is not the primary focus of this book.

Who Can Be Manipulative

While this book is called the "Narcissist's Playbook," it's important to realize that *anyone,* not just narcissists, can be manipulative. Those who manipulate on a regular basis to a destructive degree, tend to have: a personality disorder, emotional immaturity, an addiction, some sort of untreated mental illness, or a combination of the above. Manipulators come in all walks of life, and it can take some time for us to truly see their behavior clearly. Manipulators run the spectrum from parents who use guilt to control their children to a pot-stirring or otherwise difficult boss or coworker, a child predator, cult leaders, power-hungry dictators, and everything in between.

My goal isn't for you to take this information and try to diagnose the problematic people around you, or yourself. My goal is for you to understand that there are people out there whose behavior is so problematic, chronic, and long-standing that it is far outside what would be considered "normal problematic behavior." For many targets of manipulation, just the knowledge that not all problematic behavior falls within the range of workable can give them the clarity and validation they are looking for in order to distance themselves from certain people. It's not judgmental or rude to be discerning about those around you; it's healthy.

While some of the more destructive personality disorders are covered, it's important to not get hung up on the labels. The reason is that the different names and even the criteria for various diagnoses tend to change over time. So please focus on the behavior that these different diagnoses point to, as what's most important is that you see problematic behavior for what it is.

Antisocial Personality Disorder (ASPD). Formerly known as Sociopaths/Psychopaths, the antisocial personality type (ASPD) is a person who has little to no regard for social norms and rules, and is manipulative and exploitative. The term "antisocial" doesn't mean a person dislikes being social or even that they live on the fringes of society. The term "antisocial" refers to a person getting their needs met in a way that is in an anti-society, or against social norms and values, type of way. Their moral compass is in a continual state of flux based on what they want at that time. They are often hypocritical, and expect others to trust them and to treat them with honesty, loyalty, and respect, even though they refuse to treat others this way. They are often irresponsible, impulsive, entitled, and have no sincere guilt or remorse for their actions.

While all of this behavior is so problematic that we think we'd see it coming, we generally don't because many people with ASPD are charming, likable, charismatic, and social. And it's hard for many normal, decent people to comprehend that a dangerous person could be likable. Because of this, and because they know all of the right things to say, they are easily able to prey on the emotions and vulnerabilities of others and can really do a great job of acting like a wonderful person. Even for those closest to them, it might take years if not decades to fully see their pathological lying, lack of empathy and remorse, and exploitative behavior for what it is.

Compared to most narcissists, those with ASPD tend to have more self-awareness, emotional intelligence, and situational awareness to better hide their destructive behavior. Narcissists tend to be so egotistical that they never see anything wrong with their behavior and may not even try to hide it because they feel entitled to behave in whatever way they see fit. There is a lot of overlap in terms of the behaviors and mindset of those with both Narcissistic Personality Disorder and Antisocial Personality Disorder. Perhaps the best way to understand this is to realize that those with Antisocial Personality Disorder are narcissists at the core; however, not all narcissists are so extreme or exploitative that they would be considered to have Antisocial Personality Disorder.

Narcissistic Personality Disorder (NPD). Narcissists tend to have an inflated self-image and are self-absorbed to the point where they are unaware and unconcerned about the needs of others. They may expect special favors and treatment from others, are usually grandiose, think that they are special, unique, and different— sometimes to such a level that they think they are a prophet, a reincarnation of someone famous or of historical significance, or that they have a superior intellect when they don't.

They are often arrogant, entitled, manipulative, and pathological liars. When their bad behavior comes to light, their lack of insight and accountability can come across as bizarre, staggering, and even jaw-dropping—especially if they continue to lie or fake emotion in order to avoid consequences. To see this in motion is so outrageous it can be almost to the point of comical. This behavior is usually so obviously insincere to everyone but the narcissist and their staunch supporters. This can be crazy-making to see otherwise reasonable and intelligent adults defending a bunch of nonsensical behavior.

Narcissists tend to have a paper-thin ego, and any real or perceived injury to their ego can cause them to lash out in wildly inappropriate and destructive ways. They may even have a complete melt down which is basically the adult version of a temper tantrum. When this happens, they resort to name calling, screaming, and expecting others to soothe them by giving them their way. If this doesn't happen, they may throw a big enough fit that they get all that energy out of their system and by the end of it, they are somehow able to convince themselves that they've "won." There's an old joke out there about the infuriatingly immature and illogical nature of narcissists that goes, "How is arguing with a narcissist like playing chess with a pigeon?" The answer is that no matter how good you are at chess, the pigeon is just going to knock over all of the pieces, crap on the board, and strut around like it's victorious. This joke is about as accurate of a description of a narcissist's behavior as it gets.

Individuals with this personality often exaggerate (or completely fabricate) their accomplishments and talents, have a sense of entitlement, and lack empathy or concern for others. They often cannot handle any criticism and anything less than unquestioned obedience. They often use, abuse, exploit, or neglect others to get their way, and many are pathological liars. Some are parasitic in nature and mooch off friends, family, or anyone who will let them. This sense of entitlement also produces a feeling that they are allowed to punish those who do not provide their required respect, admiration, or attention. It's not uncommon for them to leave a long trail of broken-hearted targets behind them. Not all narcissists are this malicious or out-of-touch with reality. Some are more on the arrogant, difficult, subtly devaluing, self-absorbed, and standoffish end of the spectrum. However, regardless of where a person is along this spectrum, if they are unwilling to treat others with dignity and respect, there is a problem.

Those with either Narcissistic or Antisocial Personality Disorder often have two lives—reality and their fantasy life that they present to others. This fantasy life is full of excuses, manipulation, half-truths, deceptions, cons, pathological lies, and a deluded sense of self. They tend to make themselves either the hero or the victim of the stories they tell. For example, if they don't have custody or visitation with their children, they may say that the courts were against them or that their ex was abusive or manipulated the system. The reality is *they* may have been abusive, or that they don't really want anything to do with their children and don't show up to court dates. The only thing that is for certain with someone who lies is that *everything* is uncertain.

Dark Triad Personality. A Dark Triad Personality isn't a personality disorder per se; it's a destructive combination of a disordered personality (narcissism), the learned behaviors of manipulation and often sadism (Machiavellianism), and the disordered brain function of psychopathy. The result is a person who is highly manipulative, exploitative, lacking in empathy and remorse, and who enjoys causing damage and inflicting pain onto others. There is a saying out there that some people just like to watch the world burn. Those with a Dark Triad Personality would be those people.

Borderline Personality Disorder (BPD). Common characteristics of Borderline Personality Disorder (BPD) include chronic fears of abandonment, unstable social relationships, unstable self-image, attention-seeking behavior, emotional immaturity, and inappropriate or non-existent boundaries. Those with this personality disorder often engage in impulsive and self-damaging acts such as unsafe promiscuity, substance abuse, and self-harm. They tend to struggle with emotional self-regulation, experience chronic feelings of emptiness, have bouts of intense anger that are disproportionate or inappropriate to the situation, and fleeting paranoia. Those with this personality disorder tend to have an intense and chaotic life, are hypersensitive to rejection, and often have outbursts of anger as well as emotional tantrums. They may be incredibly manipulative and try to hold others emotionally hostage, often threatening suicide if they don't get their way.

A lot of the behaviors found in NPD, ASPD, and BPD overlap. It's not uncommon for a narcissist or sociopath to become dramatic, erratic, and emotional in their attempts to control their targets. However, the main difference is that people with BPD have empathy, remorse, and guilt. While they may manipulate to get their way, they aren't exploitative like a narcissist or a sociopath, and much of their behavior is more destructive to them than it is to others. If I had to wager a guess, I'd say that a lot of the most popular reality TV stars have Borderline Personality Disorder. While their antics may be entertaining to watch, if they are truly like this off camera there is a solid chance they experience a lot of pain, frustration, and sadness as a result of all of the ongoing chaos.

I want to interject here and point out that personality disorders are, at their core, a cluster of behaviors, and these behaviors, like any others, are on a spectrum ranging from mild to severe. It's important to mention this spectrum, as well as how personality disorders can (and do) manifest differently for each person. I bring this up because it's common for those who have experienced any type of abuse or trauma to be diagnosed with BPD due to their rapidly shifting moods, tumultuous relationships, and reactive, impulsive behavior. This emotional dysregulation may very well have more to do with untreated post-traumatic stress disorder (PTSD) or complex post-traumatic stress disorder (C-PTSD) both of which can be the result of trauma. The main difference between the two is that PTSD tends to occur after an event, and has more identifiable triggers, whereas C-PTSD tends to occur after repeated events, with a wider range of triggers. An example would be the difference between being a soldier in war versus being a prisoner of war. Or another way to put it would be the difference between being in a traumatic car accident and spending years in a cult. Not everyone who experiences trauma, even long-standing trauma, develops PTSD or C-PTSD; however, many do.

For a survivor of abuse, getting a diagnosis of Borderline Personality Disorder can be devastating and can further reinforce the manipulator's insistence that they were the problem. Even if a person has BPD, or any other type of personality disorder or mental illness, that doesn't make being abused somehow okay or their fault. If what I mentioned about trauma and abuse seems to more accurately describe what you went through, then I encourage you to talk to your mental health care provider about additional treatment for PTSD or C-PTSD.

The standard treatment for Borderline Personality Disorder is a therapy known as Dialectal Behavioral Therapy (DBT). This therapy is based on mindfulness and self-regulation which are valuable skills we could all benefit from.

Histrionic Personality Disorder. Those with histrionic personality disorder tend to have an excessively dramatic, overly-emotional, and attention-seeking personality. They lead with their sexuality or "bizarre-ness," and their actions tend to come across as theatrical, "over-the-top," and either immature or inappropriate—as if they aren't living in reality, but rather playing a role in a movie of their own making. They are often desperate for approval, and if anyone shows any interest in them, no matter how superficial or insincere, they are inclined to misread this as the relationship being more substantial than it is.

Addictive Personalities. When a person is struggling with addiction, they will frequently lie, deny, exploit, manipulate, threaten, and do everything in their power to make sure their addiction gets fed. It can be difficult to tell if their problematic behavior is a result of their addiction or if it's their true personality. In order to be able for you or a mental health clinician to be able to determine this, the person with the addiction would need to be sober for at least eighteen months. However, a person can have both a personality disorder and a substance use disorder. It's also possible for a person to become emotionally stunted at whatever age they first began abusing a substance.

Regardless of the source of their problematic behavior, it's okay to set boundaries with a person who has an addiction just like you would with anyone else. Having an active addiction or personality disorder might be an explanation of certain behavior, but it's not an excuse.

Character Disturbed Versus Personality Disordered

Many people get caught up on trying to figure out if the person with problematic behavior in their life has a personality disorder, and if so, which one. However, I've seen this cause more confusion than anything, as they are so focused on the trees that they lose sight of the forest. I know having a concrete diagnosis can be validating, and for many it can provide the reassurance that it's not them and that this relationship is indeed as problematic as it feels.

One of the most helpful distinctions that isn't normally made is what Dr. George Simon refers to in his book *Character Disturbance*, is that there is a difference between problematic, or even personality-disordered behavior and a "disturbed character."

A character-disturbed person is one who lacks a conscience and who has no guiding principles of right and wrong. So while some people with personality disorders may have behavior that you find exhausting, with solid boundaries on your end, this behavior could potentially be tolerable. However, if a person is character-disturbed, meaning that they have no solid moral or ethical character, but are instead guided by their selfish and destructive impulses, you would be wise to distance yourself from them. There is no healthy relationship possible with someone who lacks empathy, sincere remorse, honesty, dependability, loyalty or whose actions repeatedly harm you or others. Being around a person like this, let alone trying to establish a healthy relationship with one, will only result in chaos and *will* cost you either your safety or sanity.

This is significant, because I see a lot of people who have a loved one who might have an addiction or be diagnosed with Borderline

Personality Disorder, bipolar disorder, or even pass a psychiatric examination with flying colors, and because this person isn't officially diagnosed with a disorder that proves that they have a lack of empathy or remorse, they think this relationship can be saved. The deciding factor as to whether or not a relationship is workable needs to come from your own standards and boundaries, and nothing else. If you are being treated in a way that is not okay with you, and they can't or won't stop, then it's okay and necessary for you to set some boundaries. Keeping yourself safe and keeping peace in your life isn't being selfish, it's being self-protective.

CHAPTER 6

SUBCATEGORIES OF MANIPULATORS

From my own observations with manipulators, as well as listening to the experiences of thousands of others, I've noticed that there are six different subcategories that manipulators tend to fall into. These categories aren't hard and fast, and some manipulators may fall into more than one. Additionally, manipulators may shift between each type depending on their target and their desired outcome. The six types of manipulators are: the disorienters, the charmers, the intimidators, the martyrs, the self-harmers, and the destroyers.

The disorienter. This type of manipulator primarily uses disorientation in the form of confusion or chaos to get their way. They may play the long game by stirring the pot so they can watch it bubble over, creating chaos and then swooping in to offer a solution that benefits them. Or, perhaps, they may play the short game, creating immediate confusion so that they can knock their target off balance for some immediate gain (such as saying something cruel so that they can feel superior in that moment or with the intent to provoke the target into an explosive reaction).

Because the behavior of a disorienter is so erratic and can range from persistent to disinterested and from sweet to mean, the target is left feeling continually uncertain and anxious as to what mood they will encounter and why. In an attempt to gain understanding, the target commonly turns to the disorienter looking for clarity as to why they are now so disinterested or mean. This, of course, doesn't work and only leads to the disorienter creating more confusion, as now they know what buttons to push.

The charmer. The charmer uses charm to talk almost anyone into anything. They tend to leave a soul-mate feeling on those around them, especially if they are sexually seductive. Some of the largest amounts of damage are done by charmers, because most people don't see them coming, and those that do aren't believed. They may come across as caring, concerned, compassionate, and an overall ideal person ... at first. Over time, cracks are seen in the charmer's facade and seemingly out-of-character behavior tends to shine through. However, the reality is that this concerning behavior is the real them and the charming self that you found so compelling is an act.

The charmer may continue to hold onto their mask, continually doing damage control so that they remain to be seen as a wonderful person. The target tends to focus on the charmer being the solution, instead of seeing the charmer as the problem they really are, at least initially. Once the confusion clears, the damage that has been done can be seen.

When a relationship with a charmer ends, the target is often left trying to heal from a level of emotional devastation that they never thought possible and grieve the loss of a person they thought was their soul mate. There are four sub-types regarding the charmer: the charming charmer, the charismatic charmer, the exotic charmer, and the delusional charmer.

- **The charming charmer.** Charming charmers come across as likable, helpful, or caring, and are perhaps the most dangerous and damaging of all predators, as the best hiding place for evil is behind good. They tend to come across as caring, trustworthy, and harmless, which is how they are able to establish trust and sympathy so quickly. Those with the psychopathic behaviors of Munchausen by proxy would be a classic example of this.

  If the charming charmers are playing the short game, which is the case for online dating scammers or pick-pockets, they are quick to establish a connection which they then use to get closer emotionally or physically to their target. They may do this by using flattery, flashing a few smiles, or using casual conversation as a way to lure the target. If this happens online, the target is pulled emotionally closer through the charmer pretending to be their perfect partner. After all, a person doesn't give their life savings to an online scammer--they give it to a person they think is their significant other.

If the charmer is playing the long game, such as a spouse who chronically cheats and lies, but who wants to stay married because it's convenient for them, or if they are along the lines of the Bernie Madoffs of the world, they will finesse and reassure their target that they can be trusted. Because they lay on the charm so thick, this can leave their target feeling special and significant.

For those who have been walking around feeling unloved, lost, or lonely, the charming charmer can seem like an answer to a prayer, at least at first. Once their true intentions begin to show, the target struggles with reconciling these two different sides of this person. If they are emotionally invested in the charmer—which they usually are—they may struggle tremendously with walking away from this dynamic, as the attention, affection, or promises that everything will work out can be intoxicating. If they are in a relationship, the target may fear that they will never find someone who treats them so well or makes them feel so loved—at least when the times are good. The reality is that the charmer's over-the-top romantic behavior is all an act, and if the target doesn't realize this, then, tragically, all other relationships will fall short because normal people don't act this way. If the charmer is abusive, the target has the added challenge of knowing that others most likely won't believe them, as these charmers are seen as fantastic people.

- **The exotic charmer.** They claim to have some sort of supernatural, other-worldly or greater-than-normal abilities. They may claim to be a psychic, a prophet, a guru, an alien, or God Himself. The central theme is that they are special, unique, and different. This uniqueness holds a special type of fascination—after all, who doesn't want to talk to God, an alien, or a psychic... especially if they are feeling lost, scared, or alone. It's common for the exotic charmer to take on an exotic style of dress, an unusual name, or a unique way of life.

  The charmer tends to use this exotic appeal to then mirror the target or promise some sort of ideal future or answer. Those roped in by the exotic charmer accuse non-believers of not being open-minded. And any facts that non-believers offer up in an attempt to prove the exotic charmer is problematic or a fraud are quickly dismissed. Ironically, it's those that fall into the web of these exotic charmers who are the ones that are not open-minded. The reason this is so is because being open-minded means staying open to all possibilities being *either true or false*. It doesn't mean thinking that everything is true—especially if there is plenty of evidence that shows that this isn't the case. This isn't being open-minded, this is being gullible.

  Exotic charmers are what unbridled grandiosity looks like at its worst, and usually at its most effective. They will sell you on a dream and, in time, deliver a nightmare.

- **The delusional charmer.** The delusional and exotic charmers often go hand-in-hand. They believe that they are special, unique, different, have supernatural powers, have a direct connection to God, or that they have a connection to aliens or the dead. They may or may not actually believe in their grandiose delusions. Their bizarre beliefs appeal to those who are lost and seeking, and are leveraged in order to make money, to lure people into worshiping them, or, if they are truly mentally ill to believe in their delusions because they are so convinced they have insight that no one else has. With the delusional charmer, the more time that passes, the more bizarre and dangerous their beliefs become. Sexual abuse, child marriages, rape, murder, theft, and suicide are all spun to be necessary or righteous.

An extreme example of this would be Charles Manson, who was later diagnosed with paranoid schizophrenia (that went untreated) as well as antisocial personality disorder. The bizarre delusions and beliefs that accompany untreated schizophrenia coupled with the charisma, intensity, and manipulative behaviors of antisocial personality disorder can be a very dangerous combination. It is one that many lost, lonely, or otherwise vulnerable people seem to continually fall prey to.

The siren song of both the exotic and delusional charmer is that they often promise to know the path to being healthy, enlightened, or self-actualized. Outrageous lies and claims tend to be a long-standing pattern, and tend to be the foundation for bizarre beliefs and cult-like thinking and acting.

- **The charismatic charmer.** This person comes across as intense and persistent. They may or may not come across as charming, exotic, or delusional. Their intensity comes across as passion, and because they believe in what they are saying so sincerely, others are drawn to them. Their persistence can come across as sincerity, as this dogged determination is something that normal people only have when they are sincere. However, for a manipulative or pathological person, this persistence is about control—not caring. In their mind they need to win, and they don't let go or move on easily. For example, they may text or call numerous times—even after you've told them you don't want to see or hear from them again. They may fly across the country to apologize, show up at your home or work unannounced or uninvited, or spend large sums of money to try to win you over. You can tell the difference between pathological persistence and sincere persistence by their actions that follow. What normally happens is that once they get the target back, the target is either used, abused, exploited, or dumped. When the target is broken up with so soon after they go back to the manipulator, they are often confused because the manipulator seemed so sincere in their dogged determination to win them back. Make no mistake; they weren't. This is all a game to them.

While all abusers tend to rewrite reality on the fly and seek to destroy others around them who disagree with them, the charismatic charmer causes massive damage to massive numbers of people. On the extreme end, they may become dictators who are able to leverage strong emotions such as fear, anger, and hope in order to persuade people into doing what they want. While this is happening, those under their influence continue to minimize any concerning behavior the charismatic charmer has. After all, it's hard to spot a problem if it's either cloaked as the solution, or if we desperately want it to be the solution.

Intimidators. These manipulators intimidate targets into complying with their demands. They do this in a variety of ways such as making demeaning comments, giving the silent treatment, planting seeds of insecurity, or threatening bad outcomes if the target doesn't comply. Even though intimidators may not follow through on their threats, the threats are scary enough that the target doesn't want to risk it. These type of threats back a target into a no-win situation, and often leave them anxious and intimidated about what they should do. The target may also feel enraged at being threatened and controlled, and upset for feeling pushed into actions they don't want to take.

Destroyers/sadists. These types are the most intentional, predatory, and malicious when it comes to targeting and hurting others. They may or may not bother to build a connection with their target. Their motive is purely to destroy others, either for fun, to feed their ego, because they are bored, or simply because they can. If someone seems to enjoy causing you pain, you would be wise to immediately go into self-protective mode, and get far away from them as fast as you can.

Self-punishers. The self-punishing manipulators hold themselves emotionally or physically hostage as a way to get others to do what they want. They may threaten to start drinking, use drugs, or commit suicide if they don't get their way. They have little to no real accountability for their actions, and instead blame others. Their battle cry would be, "You made me hurt myself!"

Martyrs. The martyr-manipulator uses their considerate acts as leverage. Every kind act they do comes with strings attached and is used as an attempt to hold their target emotionally hostage with guilt down the road. They keep score by reminding the target of prior kind acts, and expect to be repaid ten-fold—and then hold it against the target if they don't. To others, they may come across as caring and concerned people who are surrounded by ungrateful people. Their main mode of manipulation could be captured in the phrase, "Look at how much I do for you."

CHAPTER 7

UNDERSTANDING THE MINDSET
OF MANIPULATORS

The motives of a manipulator may be conscious or unconscious, related to their childhood, some unhealed emotional wound, or simply to get their way. Regardless of why they are doing what they are doing, the resulting damage to you is the same if you don't move out of their destructive path. It's important that you don't let pity, sympathy, obligation, guilt, or love lead you into justifying their mistreatment of you. Spending time trying to determine what type of pathological person is in your life, or why they are treating you so terribly can feel like an important thing to do; however, what's more important is understanding how to free yourself from their manipulation and to make your safety and sanity a priority.

In addition, there's a very solid chance that you will never truly know what drives their behavior. Their intentions are often deeply rooted, have more than one cause, and can be both disguised and deflected onto others. They misrepresent their reasons for doing things. They may manipulate because it's easy, convenient, helps them to get their way, or because it's even fun for them to try and puppeteer others. Causing chaos in order to get their way may be the easiest, or most enjoyable, way to do things. So don't delude yourself into thinking that if they knew better, they would do better. Some people want to see the world burn.

Two Different Mindsets

The driving force behind a person's behavior can be traced back to one of two mindsets: domination-driven or team-oriented. Identifying the *mindset* that you are interacting with can cut through a lot of confusion. It doesn't matter if the problematic person in your life is a malignant narcissist or someone who is well-intended but emotionally immature. The core of who they are and the motives for their behavior can be difficult to determine; however, we don't need to know these things. All we need to know is what kind of mindset they have when conflict arises.

If they don't respect you or your boundaries, and if solutions-oriented communication isn't effective at solving the issue, then you aren't dealing with someone who is looking for a solution. If they deny, shift blame, lie, gaslight, or in any other way shirk accountability, then they are trying to get out of facing consequences. If you are still struggling to determine if you might be the problem, then remind yourself of all you've tried doing in order to reach a solution. If you are like any other target of manipulation, odds are you've tried everything you can think of to make the tension stop and make the relationship work, to no avail.

Here are the two different mindsets in more detail:

A Domination-Driven Mindset

A domination-driven mindset is one where a person must be in control and they must win. Any interaction with them when they don't get their way is a power struggle that leads to some sort of consequences if you don't comply. They may be difficult to please and fault finding, or bait others into arguments that never get resolved. On the more severe end, they may be sabotaging, aggressive, controlling, domineering, and unable to take criticism or competition of any kind. On the more mild end, they may be solutions-oriented in some situations, but then a switch seems to flip, they become impossible to please, and no matter what you say, they continue to bring up numerous unrelated issues that make you wrong. A person with a domination-driven mindset, even if it comes and goes, at best, is immature and has unresolved issues that only they can resolve. At worst, they have a paper-thin ego, and lash out when anyone disagrees, challenges, criticizes, or has more success than them.

A person operating from this type of mindset isn't interested in seeking a solution. They seek to "win" at all costs, even if it harms them. For example, they may continually drag their former spouse to court, racking up legal expenses for both of them, simply because they'd rather they both lose if that meant their former spouse wouldn't "win." As Steven Covey, the author of *The Seven Habits of Highly Effective People* describes it, people with a domination-driven mindset seek to have an "I win and you lose" or a "we both lose" outcome. Trying to be reasonable and work toward a solution with a person who has this type of mindset won't get you very far—in fact, it will only serve to frustrate you, upset them, and further embed them in their domination-drive to win. They would rather destroy everything around them if this means they could be King (or Queen) of the ashes.

A Team-Oriented Mindset

A team-oriented mindset is the opposite of the manipulator's domination-driven mindset. A person with a team-oriented mindset seeks to resolve issues and is able to work with others. They use honest, sincere, solutions-oriented communication to build and keep relationships. They can appropriately relate to and connect with others so that a win/win outcome is possible. Even though it might be challenging at times, they can take constructive criticism, admit faults, and moderate their behavior. They aren't threatened by the success of others. This doesn't mean that they don't get jealous, angry, frustrated, or insecure—they do, but they don't let these feelings dictate their behavior, and they don't go around sabotaging others or trying to hold them emotionally hostage.

If a person shows that they aren't team-oriented in their approach, then you are at an impasse. Now it's time to stop trying to get through to them, because ineffective communication isn't the problem. It's time to change your approach when interacting with them.

Four Main Motives of Manipulators

There are four main reasons for manipulators' behaviors:

1. To advance their selfish agenda. They want to get their way, and often disguise their motives to make this happen. They may tell you that they care, or that they are honest, that they are sorry, or that they have your best interests at heart. *Good lip service is part of the manipulation, and keeps their targets sucked in.* They may present themselves as unselfish, caring, or apologetic because it works.

2. To get and keep power and control over others. Even though manipulators may act grandiose, arrogant, or superior, they view power as finite. They can't let others be empowered because it represents less power for them. They see no room for a win/win result because they are not team oriented. If you seek to exert control over yourself or your decisions, the manipulator views it as you taking power from them. Now you've become the enemy, and they will become retaliatory to regain control.

3. To feel in control. Not getting what they want is unacceptable, and often perceived as an attack. Manipulators often want or need to be seen as in control of their emotions, especially those associated with weakness, such as anxiety, vulnerability—including bonding with others, and thus, love. They need to be right, and their egos go into a tailspin when they are wrong, disagreed with, or challenged in any way.

4. To feed their ego. Most people don't lie on a regular basis. When they do, it's generally because they are embarrassed, ashamed, feel the need to please others, or are uncomfortable with reality.

Pathological people lie and manipulate to get their way, to stir the pot, to dissolve the sanity of others, and to create chaos because it makes them feel superior, or because it's entertaining to see how much they can get someone to believe. They may lie even when the truth would work better—simply because they can or because it's fun for them to see how much they can get others to believe. If you are dealing with a pathological liar, you would be wise to assume that if they are talking they are lying. Trying to sift out fact from fiction is only an exercise in frustration. Any excuse, justification, or apology for their behavior is usually only another lie and another level to their game. Decent people may try to find underlying reasons for such terrible behavior. What we do know is that there is no relationship possible with a chronic liar, as trust, vulnerability, and honesty aren't present.

Evil Doesn't Have Rules

Regardless of their motives, it's also vitally important that you understand that if you are dealing with a malicious manipulator, you are dealing with someone who is truly evil—and *evil doesn't have rules.* This is especially the case if you are dealing with a sadistic or deadly manipulator. Nothing is sacred or off limits to them, and trying to use logic and reason to understand their behavior will get you nowhere. It's vital for you to understand that you do not share the same reality as them, or the same way of operating in this world.

The evil that you've seen up to this point is generally the tip of the iceberg. They will lie about having cancer. They will drive their supposed loved ones into bankruptcy. They may make their pets or their children sick to get attention. They will get someone pregnant (or get pregnant) to trap them. And the most damaging part is while they are causing so much harm, the targets continue to give them the benefit of the doubt and increase their support. After all, if a manipulator is making such sweeping gestures (getting married, buying a house together, quitting their job to take care of their sick child, or moving across the country to be with their target), these actions are hard to understand as being anything other than sincere. But for a manipulator, it's just another level to their game.

Malicious manipulators do not see your kindness, caring, or love as endearing; they will see it as a sign of weakness and will exploit it. There are no actions that you can take to somehow earn their love, respect, or to even be treated fairly or appropriately, although they will make you feel that there is. They will exhaust you emotionally, physically, and financially, and will not feel a sense of warmth or desire to reciprocate no matter how much you've done for them.

While past behavior is often a good indication of their future actions, there is no guarantee that their behavior won't escalate quickly, and for seemingly no reason. If someone shows you that they have a limited or absent moral compass, it's a good idea to assume that they are capable of anything. If someone has shown you that they are dangerous and destructive, it's a good idea to assume that you will see more of that in the future and that it will get worse. Manipulation and abuse go hand-in-hand, and both get worse with time, not better.

Spending time around a predator and thinking that you can either control their behavior or will be able to keep yourself safe is akin to juggling snakes--you are engaged in a dangerous past time, and just because you haven't been bit before, doesn't mean that you won't in the future. If evil is anything, it's unpredictable.

CHAPTER 8

COMMON METHODS
OF MANIPULATION

When dealing with a manipulator, it can be helpful to remind yourself that even though their hurtful behavior is currently being directed towards you, they aren't treating you this way because of something you are or something you did. A manipulative person continually creates chaos, attempts to control or exploits others because this is how they navigate life. Their behavior didn't start with you and it won't end with you. The good news is that once you understand the vocabulary for what you are experiencing, their behavior isn't as confusing and crazy-making, and it's a lot easier to disengage from it.

It's only when we don't see their behavior for what it is, and expect it to be different, that we are continually knocked off balance, shocked, and frustrated.

Common Manipulations

Some of the common manipulations are as follows:

Abusive Anger

We all experience anger. Anger is a normal human emotion, and is often experienced when we are either frustrated, feel helpless, or have had some sort of boundary crossed. However, how we deal with that anger makes all the difference. It's okay for a person to be angry, but it's not okay for them to be cruel, intimidating, or violent. Abusive anger is when one person lashes out against another. This tends to happen for three reasons: the manipulator isn't getting their way; the target acts in a way that the manipulator doesn't feel they should, or abusive anger may be a way of intimidating the target so they don't get out of line in the future. The person on the receiving end of this abusive anger often looks for rational reasons and explanations for this and may even feel responsible for causing the abusive outburst.

Example:

- You forget to respond to an important email, and your boss yells at you or tells you that you are stupid or worthless.

Blaming

Manipulators commonly blame others for their behavior and won't take any responsibility for their actions. They offer up different versions of events, as well as excuses as to why it happened, until the target either accepts one of the versions, or becomes so exhausted with the conversations that never seem to get resolved that they stop trying.

Examples:

- You find out that your partner has been having an affair, and you confront them. At first they deny it, but once you tell them that you've talked to the person with whom they cheated, they blame the other person for seducing them and they blame you for not being more sexual with them.

- You file charges against your ex for physically assaulting you, and they blame you for putting them in jail.

Boundary Pushes

Boundary pushes often happen in small, seemingly innocent ways...at least at first. For example, a date begins making offensive jokes, your mother makes a rude comment about your appearance, a coworker asks a deeply personal question about your past, or a neighbor you hardly know asks to borrow a large sum of money.

Not every person who pushes your boundaries is necessarily a manipulator. No one knows where our boundaries are until we make them clear; however, this doesn't mean that all boundary pushes are benign or accidental either. All we can do is address the boundary push when it happens, and to pay attention to how the other person responds to us holding our boundary.

When boundary pushes go unaddressed, the manipulator becomes more emboldened, as well as learns what buttons to push in the future.

Our reluctance or passivity at their boundary push, unbeknownst to the target, helps to set the pace of the dynamic.

As we become more aware of what manipulation is, and how it feels when our boundaries are crossed, this is when we are able to effectively address boundary pushes as they are happening, or at least soon after. Some people, myself included, tend to get so knocked off balance by boundary pushes that they don't know what to say or how to respond. If this is you; it's okay. Take some time to regroup, and if you can, address the boundary violation with the other person at some point in the near future, when you are ready.

Charm

When a person is charming, a common response is for people to mistake the charming person's likability for trust-ability. We tend to assign positive character traits to people who are charming, and even more so if they are attractive. Charm can be so subconsciously powerful that prosecuting attorneys often have to prepare a jury to understand that seemingly frail, female, meek, charming, or attractive people can do bad things.

Some of the most dangerous manipulators out there tend to come across as Prince (or Princess) Charming—especially when they want something. They may seem like the world's greatest parent, significant other, employee, neighbor, friend, or spiritual leader. Over time, you may begin seeing cracks in this mask, when you see them react in a way that seems really out of character for the person you think you know. Or they may be charming in public, when other people are watching, and then be very different at home. (This is why many survivors of abuse describe them as "running really hot and cold" or "Dr. Jekyll and Mr. Hyde.") Being charming is not the same thing as being a good person. After all, Bill Cosby and Ted Bundy were both very charming.

When a manipulator is being charming, they may:

- Be overly interested in you (or your children).
- Be quick to make you (or your children) their whole world.
- Give you lots of attention, affection, and compliments.
- Be quick to be the first to open up and tell you deeply intimate things about them (which may not even be true).
- Tell you that you can trust them or that they'd never hurt or cheat on you.
- Promise that given enough time, understanding, love, attention, rehab, or therapy they could change.
- Be on their best behavior, and take grand actions at saving the relationship—or offering to do whatever it takes.
- Be determined to keep you in their life, and show up at your house or work, call you continually, send you gifts, or send you an excessive amount of emails or text messages.
- Apologize, beg, plead, and cry.
- Send you songs, or write poetic texts and emails expressing their love for you, after they've cheated or abused you.

Demanding, Controlling, and Ordering

This is where one adult attempts to control what another adult will and won't do—in effect treating them like a child.

Examples:

- Your spouse insists that you never wear makeup or dress sexy when out in public—or they insist that you always wear makeup and dress sexy when out in public.

- Your spouse demands that you don't work, or that you work while they don't, and that you turn your paycheck over to them.

- Your spouse puts you on an allowance, and only gives you enough money for groceries and to put gas in your car—while they spend money however they may please.

- Your mother-in-law takes your five-year-old child to get their hair cut or ears pierced without your permission.

Emotions

The emotions of fear, obligation, guilt, and sympathy are perhaps the most preyed upon, as they are often the most effective way to get a person to comply. Here are some ways these emotions are commonly manipulated:

- **Fear.** The manipulator may threaten to end the relationship if they don't get their way—which might trigger deeper fears of abandonment, loss, or not getting what was promised such as a promotion or child support. The manipulator may become intimidating and imply they will hurt the target, children, pets, and other loved ones if the target doesn't act accordingly.

- **Obligation.** This emotion is most preyed upon in families. The pressure to submit to the manipulator's needs is cloaked under the guise of caring, or their idea of what family should do for each other regardless of the manipulator's bad behavior. For example, your sister pressures you to move your sick mother into your home, even though she's abusive to you and your children. Even if you were on good terms with her, you work full-time and don't have a spare bedroom.

- **Guilt.** The emotion of guilt often closely ties into both fear and obligation. Here are some examples of how a manipulator may use fear, obligation, and guilt. They may:

  o Blame you or others for their behavior and their problems (which can be really crazy-making if you are being blamed for them cheating, lying, stealing, etc.)

  o Use your commitment to your children against you by saying things such as, "Children need two parents," or, "I can't believe you are giving up on our marriage" when they are the ones who have had relationship-busting behavior.

  o Use religion against you, and tell you that you aren't a good person of faith because you won't let them back into your life.

  o Threaten that if you leave they won't pay child support or have anything to do with the children.

- o Promise that this time will be different and that they'll change (but their good behavior doesn't last for long, they haven't told you the full truth, or you continue to catch them in lies).
- o Promise to change, but that you are the only one who can help them.
- o Claim to have cancer or some other major illness, and that they need you to be there for them.
- o They threaten to kill you or themselves if you leave.

- **Sympathy.** If a person had a bad childhood, seems lost without us, cries, or seems physically wounded, we may be quick to discount any red flags we may have about them and replace a healthy degree of skepticism with sympathy. After all, Ted Bundy used to approach women in a parking lot wearing a cast, so that they didn't view him as the murderous threat that he was. This is because we don't fear what we pity.

Pushes for Trust that Isn't Earned

Manipulators often move fast. They target others based on what they can get, and then they prey upon their vulnerabilities and push their boundaries until the target caves in. One of the major ways this happens is a manipulator will want to combine lives in some way, such as moving in together, joining finances, having a baby, and so on.

Forgetting

This is where a manipulator claims they don't remember what

was said, or saying what did occur didn't. They may claim not remembering what they promised you. Not all people who claim to have forgotten something are necessarily lying about it. Sometimes people truly do forget. However, if you confront them about their behavior and they continue to "forget," then this is a problem.

Examples:

- You are in the middle of a big project at work, and your former spouse offers to pick up the children from daycare. Later that evening, you get a phone call from the daycare letting you know that your children are still there. You call your ex to see if they are on the way, and they tell you they forgot. Now you have to leave work early and pay a late fee as well as console two children who feel forgotten.

- Your boyfriend offers to pick you up from the airport on Saturday night. You text him on Friday to confirm and talk about how excited you are to get back home and to see him. Saturday night rolls around, and he isn't at the airport. You call him to see what's going on, and he doesn't answer. After waiting for an hour, you end up calling your sister to see if she can pick you up. You don't hear from your boyfriend until late next morning, and he tells you he forgot and then fell asleep early. You later see some pictures on social media that he was out at a bar with some friends.

Diverting, Deflection, and Blocking

Diverting and blocking are used to prevent discussion, withhold information, and end communication. When manipulators deflect, they deny their own bad behavior and instead focus on the target.

Example:

- You notice several flirtatious online messages between your partner and a coworker. When you ask your partner about it, they tell you that you have trust issues and need therapy. When you bring up the issue again, they start to point out everything you do that they don't like or they tell you that they aren't going to fight about this and shut down any further attempts you make at discussing it.

False Flattery and/or False Low Self-Esteem

Manipulators often use their charm to tell you how attractive, intelligent, or amazing you are, and how they are so lucky to have someone like you in their lives. They may point out flaws within themselves, as a way to come across as insecure and harmless.

Example:

- You start dating a new person and they tell you all about their abusive ex, and how they are afraid of being hurt again. You find yourself reassuring them that you would never treat them this way. In time, their behavior slowly shifts from them being caring, attentive, and reserved to them being difficult, demanding, and verbally abusive.

Fault Finding

When a person is continually undermined or told that everything they do is wrong, this can lead to a slow and subtle erosion of their self-esteem, leaving them to feel that nothing they do will ever be good enough, and causing them tremendous anxiety and to walk on eggshells. Over time, they may begin to doubt their abilities and judgment, and stop making decisions on their own—and instead look to the manipulator for guidance and direction.

Example:

- You have a coworker who seems to have an issue with almost everything you do. She complains that your reports are too long, and so next time you make it a point to shorten them. The next report you submit, she complains that it's too short, and so you rewrite it. Now, she has an issue with how you formatted it or with certain word choices you made. Several days later, this same coworker approaches you after lunch and says that she noticed you turn your office light off when you leave. She tells you to leave the light on because customers might think the business is closed—even though there are a dozen other offices and yours isn't visible from the road. That day you make sure to leave your light on, but when you return she has an issue with you keeping your office door closed when you aren't there.

Gaslighting

This comes from the movie Gas Lighting, which is about deception, murder, and psychological abuse. Gaslighting is a form of psychological abuse where one person intentionally and maliciously attempts to erode another's reality or sanity by saying something happened that didn't, or by saying something didn't happen that did. However, it's important to point out that denying a person's reality, even if it's done unintentionally, benignly, and with good intentions can have disastrous outcomes, which I will get into shortly.

Gaslighting is done in four main ways, for four very different reasons. However, regardless of the intent, there are still profound negative consequences to the person on the receiving end of it.

These four ways and reasons are:

1. A person denies reality <u>in order to avoid consequences.</u>

<u>Example</u>: Emily discovers her husband, Brandon, has been having an affair. When she confronts him, he denies it and tells her she is paranoid and crazy for even thinking he would cheat on her.

<u>Likely intention:</u> Brandon may be denying reality in an attempt to avoid consequences.

<u>Consequence:</u> While Brandon may not be intending to erode Emily's sanity, that is frequently the result when someone is told they are wrong about reality, when they aren't. The person on the receiving end of this form of gaslighting tends to have difficulty trusting their judgment and other people, long after the manipulator is out of their life.

2. A person denies reality <u>in order to intentionally erode the sanity of another.</u>

<u>Example:</u> Charlotte is jealous that Diana, her "friend" and fellow coworker, got a raise last month when she didn't. Over the past month, Charlotte has been periodically going to Diana's office and deleting files off of her computer. Because Diana thought Charlotte was a friend, she confides in her that some important files are missing, and she has no idea how this could have happened. Charlotte

tells her she's under a lot of stress and must have misplaced them. A week later, Charlotte begins telling Diana misinformation about certain projects that causes Diana to lose those clients. When Diana confronts Charlotte about this misinformation, Charlotte acts shocked, and says that she never said any of that. She goes on to tell Diana that as her friend, she recommends that she sees a doctor because she's concerned Diana is having a nervous breakdown.

Likely intention: Charlotte is intentionally trying to erode Diana's sanity.

Consequence: If Diana doesn't realize Charlotte is behind all of the chaos and confusion, Charlotte might continue toying with her to the point where Diana begins seeing a doctor for anxiety or depression. Things may even get so bad that Diana is unable to keep her job or does end up having a nervous breakdown.

Even if Diana realizes what Charlotte has been up to, she may feel suspicious and distrusting of others.

3. A person denies reality because <u>they don't understand the reality of another.</u> This type of unintentional gaslighting can happen with mental health clinicians or police. For example, Sharon is in an emotionally and psychologically abusive relationship but doesn't realize it—she just thinks her relationship is complicated, and fears she is to blame as her boyfriend continually has issues with her appearance, her hobbies and friends, and her opinions on most things. When he gets upset, he either yells and calls her names or he gives her the silent treatment. When she brings up these issues with her therapist, she is overly sensitive because her mother was hyper-critical of her when she was a child. Another example would be if someone were being stalked by an ex, or if the ex was harassing them by coming to their work, leaving gifts on their doorstep, or continuing to call them from blocked numbers, and the police were to say that these are all signs that their ex cares about them.

4. A person denies reality <u>in order to ease their anxiety about it.</u> This fourth form of gaslighting isn't what most people think of when they think of gaslighting or psychological abuse. However, *out of all the forms, this one is perhaps the most damaging because it is so common, seen as no big deal, and yet is so incredibly corrosive.* In fact, it can be a major reason as to why people get and stay tangled up with manipulators.

Example #1: A child falls down and scrapes his elbow. His mother rushes over, kisses his elbow, and tells him that he is "all better."

Example #2: A child wants to try a new food, and their older sibling tells them that they won't like it, and convinces them to eat something else.

Example #3: A child is uncomfortable around a certain relative, and their grandparent tells them that they are being silly or difficult and to go give that person a hug or sit on their lap.

Possible intention: These intentions are usually good, and are meant to either soothe the child, look out for them, or teach them manners. However, no matter how well-intended we might be, whenever we insist that someone's thoughts or feelings are wrong, we are separating them from their reality.

Consequence: The result of a child having their reality denied is that they don't learn how to correctly interpret the messages their emotions are trying to send. Or, if this kind of invalidation is chronic, the child disconnects from certain emotions, such as hurt, sadness, or anger completely. As this child becomes an adult, they will most likely struggle with uncertainty and indecisiveness because they don't know how they feel or what they like or don't like. They often don't know when they are in emotional or physical pain, and in terms of relationships, they don't know when they are being mistreated, or how to respond if they are. They are quick to assume they are wrong and look to others for validation.

Minimizing and Invalidating

Minimizing and invalidating occur when the target's concerns are discounted or denied. This is usually done by blaming the target for being too sensitive, too emotional, unable to take a joke, twisting things around, looking for a fight, making a big deal out of nothing, being crazy, losing their hearing or memory, bringing up everything the target has ever done wrong, or accusing the target of bringing up these issues because the target has major issues with commitment. What can be confusing here is that some points may contain nuggets of truth; the target may have issues with trust, for example. However, that doesn't change the fact that the manipulator is acting in ways that are untrustworthy.

Hoovering

Hoovering is a manipulation technique named after the Hoover vacuum, where the manipulator attempts to suck the target back into the relationship. The manipulator's attempts at reopening communication may seem harmless, such as them saying "hello" or "happy birthday" or texting out of the blue. They may also claim that they are terminally ill, that they are suicidal, that they are going to be homeless and need a place to stay, and so on. Most normal, decent people that are on the receiving end of this kind of behavior tend to feel rude if they don't respond. Manipulators are relying on you to feel this way, so don't fall for it. Additionally, expect their failed attempts at communicating with you to escalate and to switch from sweet to mean or from mean to sweet. Remember, they are trying to bait or provoke you into responding. It's all a game to them—a game they are trying to win. Don't mistake their persistence as anything other than this. And please know that cutting off communication isn't about punishing the manipulator; it's about taking the actions necessary to protect yourself.

Intimidation

A manipulator can be intimidating in direct or indirect ways. It may be their tone of voice, certain words that they choose, or an icy chill when they walk into the room. They may be physically intimidating in ways such as towering over a person, shoving, standing too close, shouting, or stalking.

Isolation

Isolation is the number-one tool in a manipulator's tool kit. Manipulation works best when the target doesn't have another person around who can validate or inform them that what they are experiencing is, indeed, problematic. The manipulator may:

- Create a "you and me versus the world" dynamic, where others don't understand how much the two of you have been through, when really it's that the manipulator has put you through so much.

- Separates the target from anyone who doesn't support them staying together.

- Pressure the target to spend less time with friends and family— especially if the target's support system sees how the target is being mistreated.

- Pressure you to spend all of your time with them or talking to them.

- Pressure you to move in with them or move to another city, state, or country to be with them.

- Pressure you to quit your job so that they know where you are at all times.

If the manipulator is showering the target with attention and affection, the target may willingly and unknowingly isolate themselves from others by spending all their time with the manipulator. The target may also distance themselves from their friends and family out of shame for how they're being treated or friends and family may distance themselves from the target because they're frustrated and tired of spending time and energy supporting the target in their efforts to leave, only to have the target return a week later.

Lying

Lying tends to go hand-in-hand with manipulation. The manipulator may play the victim or they may come up with stories that are complete fabrications. When these lies find their way back to the target, the target is usually shocked and confused as to how or why they could say such outrageous things.

Love Bombing

Love bombing is excessive communication, compliments, and future faking to lure a target into (or back into) a relationship. When this happens, the target may feel uneasy with all this attention and affection as though it is too much too soon. If the target mistakes this love bombing for sincere interest, it can lead to them falling hard and fast for the manipulator. Once this attention and affection dry up, the target does anything to get it back.

Love bombing is something that is primarily associated with cults and online dating scammers, but it can happen with manipulators of any kind. This level of attention isn't sincere—it's sinister. What can seem like caring behavior at first, soon shows itself to be controlling. It can feel intoxicating to feel so loved and accepted, especially if a person has been feeling lonely or unloved for any length of time.

Mirroring

Mirroring, to an extent, is a normal thing that we all subconsciously do when we are trying to connect with another person.

Mirroring is when we reflect (mirror) back elements of the people that we are around. However, a manipulator may intentionally mirror their target's style of dress, word usage, religion or spirituality, morals, values, hopes, dreams, and even fears as a way of connecting with the target and creating a false sense of security and soul-mate type of connection. Those being mirrored may have a hard time walking away from (and "getting over" a relationship with) a manipulator because of this intense connection, not realizing this connection was never real.

Needling and Baiting

Needling and baiting is when one person pokes (needles) at another person's sensitive issues as a way of baiting them into an explosive reaction or an argument. The manipulator will then often sit back and either claim innocence or use the highly-reactive behavior of their target as proof that the target is the one with the issues. This leaves the target wondering if they really are the problem.

Projection

Projection is when one person projects their uncomfortable thoughts, feelings, or actions onto another to relieve their discomfort. Manipulators are notorious for doing this. Being accused of things you aren't doing is incredibly confusing, and leaves a target questioning their recollection of events and their sanity. Manipulators commonly accuse their targets of cheating, lying, stealing, being abusive, being manipulative and anything else the manipulator has done or is doing. When manipulators do this—watch out. They have now done the mental gymnastics necessary to make themselves the victim of you. And in their mind, any aggressive actions they now take are in self-defense.

To be on the receiving end of this can be absolutely crazy-making and the target may start going to great lengths to hold onto their sanity. They may start writing down or recording conversations, taking pictures of text messages, or taking screen shots of what they find online. However, no matter how much proof they have, the manipulator won't ever be fully accountable for their behavior.

Put-Downs Disguised as Jokes or "Brutal" Honesty

It's common for manipulators to grind away at a target's self-esteem any way they can. The use of put-downs, mean jokes, or brutal honesty is a common way they do this. The manipulator may make comments such as, "Your butt is the size of a barn;" or, "You are easily entertained." If the target gets upset, the manipulator then claims they were just joking. (And even if they are, if you tell someone you don't like "jokes" like that, and they keep it up, then they don't respect your boundaries—and this is a problem.) Over time, these kinds of comments erode the target's self-esteem making them more vulnerable to future, and often more severe, manipulation.

Rushing Intimacy

Manipulators move fast and rush intimacy by getting targets to share their deepest desires, fears, and insecurities to later use against them. They are quick to talk about love, getting engaged, getting married, and combining their lives. Because the soul-mate connection established during the love bombing is reinforced with the mirroring and then further fueled with this rushed intimacy, targets often think they've found an amazing person.

Subtle Attacks

Subtle attacks are when seeds of jealousy or insecurity are planted within the target or others around the target. These attacks are done in such a way that the target and those around them don't see them for what they are. For example, if a manipulator is trying to smear their ex's reputation or instill uncertainty in the minds of others they may say something such as, "I want to be civil about our divorce. I don't want to bring up her drinking or her untreated bipolar disorder." These attacks often have nothing to do with reality and paint the target as unstable.

Another way the manipulator uses subtle attacks is in trying to cause the target to feel jealous or insecure. The manipulator may start flirting with others, or tell the target about how others flirt with the manipulator. Even to a target who isn't normally jealous or insecure, being on the receiving end of these kinds of comments can put them on edge.

Threatening

Threatening behavior is when a manipulator threatens a partner by going after their biggest fears—usually pulling away whatever safety the target is craving. Manipulators may threaten in both overt and covert ways to break up, or file for divorce, not pay child support, not see their children, not give that promotion, not leave you alone, etc. The implication is made clear, "Do what I want or else."

Triangulating/Pot Stirring

Triangulation is when there are three people involved in a two-person situation. Manipulators are notorious for using triangulation to create chaos. This is done by the manipulator putting themselves in the middle and pitting two other people against each other by feeding each of them lies, half-truths, gossip, or private information about the other. The result of triangulation is division between the two people being pitted against each other, with fighting soon to follow.

Example:

- You recently had a baby and are self-conscious about your body. Your partner knows this, and is continually mentioning how attractive and in-shape his new coworker is—and that maybe he could ask her for some pointers for you.

Undermining

Undermining behavior is where the manipulator continually points out everything wrong with the target's ideas or decisions, and often includes withholding emotional support as a result. For example, if the target decides to get into real estate investing, the manipulator may talk about how terrible the market is, or how they will never succeed. If the target goes to college, the manipulator may criticize the choice of majors. Or, perhaps, the target may want to send the children to summer camp, but the manipulator will list everything wrong with the camp or why the children shouldn't go. The main theme is that whatever the target wants to do that the manipulator doesn't agree with, the manipulator will sabotage their efforts. The result is that the target loses faith in their decision making abilities and, instead, turns to the manipulator for guidance.

Violence

A manipulator may become violent or threaten violence in direct or indirect ways. They may start yelling, cussing, or be physically intimidating such as throwing things at or around the target. They may also post indirect or direct threats on social media that are geared to either intimidate the target or rile up others to harassing or attacking the target as well.

Virtue Signaling

This is when a person posts online or goes to great lengths in person to point out how virtuous of a person they are. I heard a great quote the other day that beautifully sums up the concept of virtue signaling. "If you want to feed the homeless, feed the homeless. If you want to post about how you fed the homeless on social media, then you are feeding your ego." Abusers and manipulators often love to virtue signal because it's an easy way for them to look like a good person. They may have a tattoo of their child's name, or pictures of their child all over their social media, but may rarely see them or pay child support. They may participate in walks against domestic violence, when the reality is they are physically abusive to their spouse. They may talk at great length how they value commitment, while they are cheating. The hypocrisy can be jaw-dropping.

Wearing down the Target

When a manipulator attempts to wear down their target, it's usually because they want to have the last word in an argument or they want to exhaust the efforts of the target. For example, the manipulator might try to wear down the target's boundaries, patience, or finances, such as by continually dragging the target to court for frivolous matters, causing the target to take time off work or to pay for child care and/or legal expenses.

The manipulator may launch into a lengthy argument in defense of their behavior that is generally repetitive, circular, veers off track, lacks any sense of sincere accountability or resolution, and shifts to focus on everything wrong with the target. The result is that the target winds up being frustrated, worn out, and sorry they ever brought up any issues in the first place.

A more overt form of wearing down a target happens within cults and high-pressure sales pitches. Both groups will often keep people in a room for long periods of time denying them use of the bathroom, food, sleep, and access to others who weren't in support of them enrolling. This pressure is cloaked in such a way that other people who don't agree with their beliefs or sales pitch are painted as an ignorant or negative force that's holding them back. In reality, the target's vulnerabilities are being exploited as they are continually being fed a seduction story of how great their life will be once they join. If the target has questions or wants to leave, they are often shamed, threatened with abandonment (as is the case of cults who disown former members), or pressured into meeting with higher-ranking members who are able to convince them to stay.

Weasel Wording/Use of Euphemisms

Weasel wording is when a manipulator chooses their words very carefully, often to either soften or deny the reality of a situation. For example, a manipulator may claim that they *would never* abuse or cheat on their partner, but this isn't the same as saying that they *haven't ever* abused or cheated on their partner. Shifting the focus from past events to what might happen in the future absolves them of guilt and accountability.

Another spin is to be very selective about the meaning of one word. For example, they may say that they never had a relationship with a certain person, even though they've had sex with them. What really may have happened is that they had sex with that person, but in their mind it wasn't a relationship, so they spin things to where they feel they've answered honestly.

When manipulators answer in such a selective way, the target can feel like they are trying to drag the truth out of them, because they are. And then it's the target who becomes exhausted with attempting to select the exact, right words in order to get to the truth. Of course, the manipulator may play dumb and act as though the target is the one with poor communication, and that they would have answered the question differently had the target been more clear. Make no mistake, if you were to answer their questions in this way, they'd be infuriated because a manipulator does not feel that you are entitled to treat them as they treat you.

Withholding

Manipulators may withhold important information, affection, attention, or communication. The manipulator may withhold certain important information such as phone messages, days and times of important appointments, important health information that their partner needs to know such as sexually transmitted infections, phone messages, and so on. They may make statements such as, "There's nothing for me to say." "You don't deserve to know," or, "You never asked."

CHAPTER 9

UNDERSTANDING CRAZY-MAKING CONVERSATIONS

The previous chapter covered common manipulative and abusive behavior. However, it's also important to understand *why* so many of the conversations that go along with these behaviors are so confusing and crazy-making. One of the main reasons conversations with narcissists, and many other manipulators, are so infuriating is because their communication—especially their justifications for their behavior—tends to be irrational and illogical. This is because it's a reflection and expression of their world view and emotional immaturity. Odds are you've had conversations with a manipulator where they've said something so nonsensical or outrageous that your jaw literally dropped open. You may have been left wondering how their thinking could possibly be so skewed, let alone how they could say something so wildly problematic out loud and think that what they are saying would sound reasonable to anyone else. Or, you may have been left feeling that the failure to understand is yours—that you can't communicate effectively for some reason. Perhaps you may feel that you really are the difficult one, or, if you've been in an emotionally and psychologically abusive relationship before, that you misinterpret everything they say due to your past unresolved issues. This is especially the case if your past abuse was more overt, such as name calling and yelling. Whereas this person is being passive-aggressive by using sarcasm, a condescending tone of voice, hurtful jokes, or other such subtle slights that they could easily deny and put back on you for being too sensitive.

When people are being manipulative, they usually attempt to justify their behavior, avoid the truth, or shirk accountability by blaming others. These attempts often result in what's known as "word salad" which is a series of responses all tossed together that don't seem to make any sense and only serve to further derail the conversation. In order to better understand word salad, it can help to get familiar with the concept of "logical fallacies." The term logical fallacy means false logic, or an error in reasoning, and is the foundation of philosophy and critical thinking. These errors in reasoning aren't always intentional or meant to be manipulative--any of us can fall into making them or being persuaded by them. However, whenever faulty reasoning is being used, a logical conclusion is difficult to reach. What makes for an error in thinking is that the premise of what someone is asserting doesn't support or line up with the conclusion they are reaching. This is known in philosophy as a "non-sequitur" which is Latin for "it does not follow." The result of this is a derailed conversation.

Conversations with manipulators tend to really get crazy-making when they start using a combination of logical fallacies. This is often why a target struggles with pinpointing what happened and why their dynamic with this person is so confusing. Becoming familiar with common logical fallacies will help you understand why certain conversations are so maddening and give you the validation needed that the issue isn't with you or your communication. Additionally, you will also be able to be able to strengthen how you analyze information, especially when it comes to telling the difference between solid reasoning or advice, and unsound reasoning or well-intended bad advice.

This chapter only covers some of the main errors in reasoning, used by both manipulators and their targets, that I've most frequently observed. A more complete list with examples can be found on my website at: www.thriveafterabuse.com/crazymakingconversations. The following list, and the concept of logical fallacies in general, might seem complex, and in many ways they are. The goal of this chapter is to simply give an overview of breakdowns in communication.

9 Frequently-Used Errors in Reasoning (Logical Fallacies)

1. The Pollyanna Principle. This error in reasoning is made when a person thinks that others have the same morals and motivations that they do. A twist on this line of thinking is that if other people don't have the same morals and motivations that you do, that they would, if only they had or have the same set of circumstances. The Pollyanna Principle is one that targets of manipulators often make. This fallacy contributes to crazy-making conversations in that the target assumes that the manipulator's communication is sincere, mature, and an attempt to keep a good relationship going, not realizing that the manipulator is consciously or unconsciously trying to get and keep control by shifting the conversation off-course in some way.

Some of the faulty thinking that stems from the Pollyanna Principle is:

- *Other people will treat me like I treat them.*
- *If I do good things, good things will happen to me.*
- *Surely they didn't mean to say or do such a hurtful thing.*
- *They can't intentionally be trying to start an argument, because I can't see any reason for us to argue.*

This is faulty thinking because not everyone has the same set of morals and motivations that you do, and if a person has malicious intentions towards you, then it's important you see their behavior for what it is—and not through the lens of your own understanding of how people should or will behave. The Pollyanna Principle is what drives the thoughts and actions of many normal, decent people who stay with or support manipulative people.

The only way that you can appropriately and effectively treat others as the individuals that they are is to see them as such, and to not see them as a broken version of you. Fully understanding this may just save your life someday.

2. Appeal to Ignorance. This fallacy is used when someone bases the validity of a statement based on a lack of evidence. The thinking is that something must be true because there is no evidence proving otherwise. The thinking behind this is that if you can't prove it, then it didn't happen.

Examples:

- *Sarah's boyfriend tells her that she can't prove he was cheating; therefore, he didn't cheat.*
- *No one has ever caught Tina stealing, therefore she can be trusted.*
- *OJ Simpson was found not guilty of killing Nicole Brown and Ron Goldman this means he didn't do it.*

Just because Sarah can't prove her boyfriend cheated, doesn't mean he didn't cheat; it just means that Sarah isn't able to prove it. And while no one has ever caught Tina stealing doesn't mean she can be trusted, it just means that no one has ever caught her stealing--not to mention that there are numerous other things she could do, besides steal, that would make her untrustworthy. Additionally, just because OJ Simpson was found not guilty in criminal court doesn't necessarily mean he didn't murder Nicole Brown and Ron Goldman. It meant that there wasn't enough evidence for a jury to find him guilty beyond a reasonable doubt based on the evidence presented. (OJ Simpson was later found guilty of these two murders in civil court.)

3. Appeal to hypocrisy. This fallacy is when a person shifts the focus onto the other person's wrong doings as a way to defend their own behavior. This might be best understood as, "Your wrong doings absolve me of my wrong doings."

Example:

- *Paul gets pulled over by the police for driving under the influence of alcohol. When his father finds out, he begins to tell Paul about the dangers of drinking and driving. Paul tells his father that he can't tell him not to drink and drive when his father has also been in trouble for driving under the influence.*

While his father's behavior is hypocritical and annoying to Paul, just because his father drinks and drives doesn't make Paul's drinking and driving okay; additionally, the dangers of drinking and driving that his father brings up are still valid.

A broader application of this fallacy would be "I did this because you did that" or that two wrongs should make a right. A lot of passive-aggressive and aggressive behavior falls into this category. An example of this fallacy as it pertains to passive-aggressive behavior would be if a person was promised a raise but never given one, and then feels justified for not clocking out for lunches, or saying that they worked more hours than they did, as a way to get paid more.

In terms of abusive behavior, this fallacy is used to support the justification, "Look at what you made me do." Here's an example:

- *Sonya forgot to take her car in for an oil change and now the light is on. When her father finds out, he yells at her, telling her that she is stupid and incapable of being responsible. She begins to cry, at which point her father gets upset and says that she only has herself to blame--that he doesn't like having to yell and call her names, but because she forgot to get her oil changed he had no choice but to yell and insult her.*

The reality is that her mistake doesn't justify her father's abusive behavior. While he might be upset with her, there are many others way he could address the situation without becoming abusive.

The other way that this error in reasoning is used by those with abusive behavior is by thinking that the target can't hold the abuser accountable for their problematic behavior if the target has ever done anything *either real or perceived* the abuser has ever had a problem with. When a person has this train of thinking, situations can escalate quickly and without warning, because while the abuser may think they've been wronged, they haven't--this injustice only occurred in their mind. This is due their distorted world view which dictates that they are right and everyone else is wrong. The result of this thinking is they expect other people to think, feel, and act a certain way, and if they don't, then they are justified in abusing them. Targets frequently attempt to "do better" and be more of what the abuser wants in order to avoid being punished in some way. However, this never works for long as the abuser's expectations are ever-shifting, and they expect targets to read the abuser's mind and, therefore, to somehow know when they've done something that's not okay with the abuser. Even if the target was given a list of things to do and not do, and could follow it perfectly, and this stopped the abuse (which it still wouldn't), the result would be that they would have lost much of what makes them an individual in their efforts to appease the abuser.

Examples:

- *Betty comes home with a new haircut. Her husband flies into a rage, accusing her of trying to make herself look more attractive for other men. (Betty's husband feels entitled to lash out at her because in his mind she's trying to get the attention of other men. This kind of thinking and behaving is common for abusive people, as they expect the target to always act in a way that they see fit, and if the target doesn't, the abuser takes this as a personal attack when it's not—it's simply the target being an individual.)*

- *Sasha and Ryan are dating. He finds out she's cheating on him. When he confronts her, she says that he can't get mad at her for cheating on him because he's gained weight.*

4. Blaming the Victim. This is when the abuser blames the victim (or target) for being abused or for actions the abuser takes. In terms of manipulation, this strategy is often used to hold a victim/target emotionally hostage.

Examples:

- *If you don't get back together with me, I'm going to kill myself and it will be all your fault!*

- *You forgot to buy cat food at the store, that's why I yelled at you.*

- *I told you that I would kill you if you ever tried to leave me. You tried to leave me, and I beat you up, and now I have to go to prison for what you made me do?! This is all your fault; you ruined my life.*

5. Appeal to Emotion. This is when someone manipulates the emotions of another to get their way. Some of the emotions most commonly appealed to are guilt, pity, fear, and anger. This error in reasoning is different from "blaming the victim" in that blaming someone else for the actions of another/the abuser is the issue whereas with an appeal to emotion, a person isn't necessarily blaming them, but they are attempting to make them feel a certain way. Many manipulators know that if they get loud or otherwise become aggressive, those around them who don't like conflict will tend to fall in line. This is so effective that many trial lawyers are taught this rule: If you have the facts, pound on the facts. If you have the law, pound on the law. If you don't have either, pound on the table. Using aggression is a way to seize control of the situation by knocking others off center, as well as intimidating others into complying.

Examples:

- *If you loved me, you would give me another chance.*
- *I know you have a restraining order against me, but I just found out I have cancer and need to talk to you.*
- *A wife files for divorce from her abusive husband. He responds by telling her that she's selfish and needs to think about the children.*

6. Continuum fallacy. This fallacy comes from thinking that if two things exist on a continuum, then there no definable point at which these two things meet, then these things are the same. For example, since human behavior exists on a continuum ranging from functional to profoundly dysfunctional, and we all have behaviors peppered along this continuum, then no one's behavior is better or worse than someone else's. While it may be true that behavior is never 100 percent functional or dysfunctional, there are still behaviors that are more functional or dysfunctional than others. The phrase "No one is perfect" is often a reflection of the continuum fallacy since no one's behavior is 100 percent bad or good, then we shouldn't have an issue with someone's behavior, because we aren't perfect either.

Example: Zoe confronts Logan about several lies that she's caught him in. He gets upset, tells her she's crazy, and then breaks up with her. Zoe is upset, but she realizes this is for the best, and that she needs to move on. Later that night, Logan starts texting her saying that he'll forgive her for accusing him of lying. He goes on to gaslight her and plant seeds of insecurity by saying that he loves her even if she's crazy and jealous. Zoe says that she is done and tells Logan to not call her anymore. Logan gets upset and begins pointing out all of the mistakes Zoe has made as well as telling her that she thinks she's better than him, but she shouldn't, as her nose is big, her new haircut looks stupid, and she's out of shape so she's not as perfect as she thinks. Zoe doesn't fall for this and tells Logan again that she doesn't want to see him anymore and to leave her alone. She then hangs up the phone and blocks Logan's number.

While no one is perfect, this doesn't mean that all behavior needs to be tolerated. We can still be imperfect people and have boundaries and deal breakers.

7. Appeal to Intuition. This is where someone uses their intuition as a measure of whether something is true or not.

Example #1: Suzy files a report with Diana, the head of the human resources department of her company, claiming that her boss, Brian, is sexually harassing her. After Suzy leaves, Diana shreds the report because she's never had a bad feeling from Brian, and therefore he couldn't be sexually harassing Suzy.

This is an error in thinking because Diana is substituting her intuition about Brian as truth, instead of realizing this is her subjective experience with him and not proof of his behavior towards others.

Example #2: Lisa doesn't want to go out on a second date with Ted because she has an unsettling feeling about him.

The reason Lisa's instincts or intuition *are not* an error in reasoning in this situation, because she's not asserting that her instincts about Ted are the truth. She doesn't want to go out on a date with Ted because there's something about him that makes her feel uncomfortable, and feeling uncomfortable around someone is a valid reason to not go out on another date. If Lisa were to say that she doesn't want to go out on a second date with Ted because her instincts tell her that he's a serial killer, then this would be more debatable as we don't know if Ted is in fact a serial killer. However, it's still okay for Lisa to not want to go on a second date with him.

8. Hasty Generalization. This is when a large generalization is made based on a small amount of information.

Example #1: The last three men I dated all cheated on me, therefore, all men are cheaters.

Example #2: Every friend I've ever had that's betrayed my trust has been a Scorpio, therefore all Scorpios are manipulative and can't be trusted.

Example #3: All blondes have more fun; all brunettes are serious; and red heads are nothing but trouble.

In all three of these examples, a generalization is based on a small amount of information. Targets of abuse commonly fall into this error in thinking when they go about trying to avoid manipulators. When a person doesn't see problematic behavior as the problem, they are prone to linking up all kinds of incorrect cause and effect and making hasty generalizations like the ones listed above.

9. Red Herring. Historically, a red herring was a strong-smelling fish that was used by hunters (or criminals) to throw bloodhounds off of their scent. The term is now used to describe when someone attempts to distract from the topic at hand, resulting in the conversation going completely off-track.

Example:

John comes home from the bar at four in the morning. Sandra, his wife, gets upset and asks him why he's home so late. John responds that Sandra came home late last night, and so she has no right to be upset. (Appeal to hypocrisy.) Sandra replies that she came home at seven in the evening, not at four in the morning, and the reason she came home late was because she had a meeting that ran over. John says that he doesn't know that for certain, and that maybe Sandra is actually cheating on him. Confused by John's insinuation that she might be cheating, she begins to defend herself...and the topic is now focused on Sandra.

Remember, if a manipulator is looking to avoid accountability or get their way, they aren't looking to work with facts or be held accountable. When a person is engaging in illogical thinking, attempting to stay logical and keep the conversation on topic usually results in annoying them and frustrating yourself. Additionally, if you point out to a manipulator how they are being irrational, they may take this as an attack and become even more aggressive or violent.

CHAPTER 10

THE DIFFERENT LEVELS OF MANIPULATIVE BEHAVIOR

Learning about the common methods of manipulation often brings about the first few rays of light to pierce through the confusion. Becoming aware of the different categories of manipulative behavior and the various ways it comes across lifts that fog even more. Manipulative behavior tends to fall within three main categories: crazy-making, destructive, and dangerous.

Crazy-Making Behavior

Crazy-making behavior is behavior that can result in even the calmest person losing their cool, and behaving in ways they normally don't. What makes crazy-making behavior so enraging and exhausting is that's it's immature, illogical, irrational and stays that way. There isn't anything a target can say or do to bring about a mature, logical, rational, or solutions-oriented discussion. Crazy-making behavior often involves:

- Continual blame shifting, the attacker making themselves into the victim
- Denial of facts (gaslighting)
- Disengaging from communication, or refusing to address the issue at hand (stonewalling)
- Deflection of the issue at hand (usually by focusing on things other people or you have done wrong)
- Outrageous lies and accusations
- An unwarranted sense of righteousness or anger on the crazy-maker's end
- A lack of accountability
- A frustrating and infuriating level of selfishness, immaturity, and cruel indifference
- Hypocritical behavior. All expectations are a one-way street. They expect you to treat them with loyalty, honesty, and respect, but don't see why they should treat you or others the same way.

Destructive Behavior

I'm using the term "destructive behavior" to refer to relationship-destroying behavior, not physically destructive behavior. Physically aggressive behavior is covered in the next section. Relationship-destroying behavior involves the immaturity and lack of accountability that is found in crazy-making, but also includes major breaches of trust. Some examples of relationship-destroying behavior are:

- **History of financially exploitative actions.** For example, stealing, intentionally mismanaging household funds, opening up credit cards, utility bills, or taking on debt that another person is responsible for without their knowledge or approval.

- **History of emotionally unsafe actions, such as:**

- **Threatening to end the relationship as punishment.** For example, a pattern of breaking up or threatening divorce whenever they don't get their way. The result is that the target never knows how stable the relationship is, treads lightly in order to avoid causing any upset, and feels perpetually anxious.

- **Ending the relationship seemingly out of nowhere.** This is usually done as either a punishment or if they want to cheat and are trying to absolve themselves of any guilt for doing so. When this happens, the target doesn't usually find out until later that they've had sex with someone else, and once this is discovered, the manipulator will say that they were broken up at the time.

- **Ongoing "squirrelly" behavior.** For example, a person acting in a suspicious way, such as hiding their phone, giving vague answers, befriending sexy strangers on social media, disappearing for hours on end and refusing to say where they went, or shutting down any attempts at discussing their concerning behavior. This kind of behavior creates a break in trust, as it should. People who sincerely want to be in a relationship don't have squirrelly behavior. If they happen to do something that their partner has an issue with, they are open to discussing it and working towards a resolution. Targets may think that because they don't have concrete proof that anything is going on that if they broke up over this, that they'd be overreacting. This is untrue. A fulfilling relationship requires honesty, trust, emotional safety, and true intimacy. If any one of these are missing, there is no deep relationship possible.

- **Cheating.** When a person cheats, all trust and connection are destroyed. If any relationship is possible after this, then it is up to the person who cheated to do the work of repairing the relationship and proving that they can be trusted. This will take years, if not decades.

- **History of using your past against you.** For example, deeply personal things that you have told them are later used against you when they are angry. (Them getting angry isn't the same thing as a fight between two people. When two people in a relationship fight, there is a more legitimate cause, and both people are angry and upset. Manipulators and targets don't often get into a fight—it's more that the manipulator becomes angry, or manufactures an upset as an excuse to lash out or punish their target, and all the target can do is to try and diffuse things.)

- **Erratic and emotionally hurtful behavior.** Their behavior may run hot and cold, as though they have a Dr. Jekyll and Mr. Hyde type of personality. When the hurtful Mr. Hyde side comes out, their actions show that they don't have good intentions, let alone your best intentions in mind.

Dangerous Behavior

Dangerous behavior often includes crazy-making and relationship-busting behavior; however, due to intimidation and aggression, their behavior is now at a whole new and dangerous level. Those with dangerous behavior often have a quick temper, escalate quickly, and have a pattern of reacting in an aggressive, violent, erratic, or impulsive way when they want something, are disagreed with or challenged, when they don't get their way, or if they want to punish the target for some perceived injustice.

This kind of behavior needs to be taken seriously, regardless of whether or not this is normal behavior for them, or if you've experienced worse from someone else.

A person who sees no problem with their aggressive or violent behavior and who lacks respect for the rights of others is dangerous. I can't stress this last point enough. It's very common for those with an aggressive person in their lives to get so used to explosive outbursts that their ability to discern when they are in harm's way becomes skewed. The result is that they don't realize how dangerous this situation is or when to move themselves to safety. *These are the kinds of dynamics that often end in murder or murder-suicide.*

Some examples of dangerous and deadly behavior include:

- Aggressive, violent, sadistic, or deadly behavior towards animals, you, or others.

- Use of fear, intimidation, or violence to get you to comply, often threatening to hurt you or those you care about.

- A history of restraining orders or jail time for domestic violence, stalking, or violent crimes.

- A history of behavior that shows a jaw-dropping lack of remorse, respect, or empathy towards others.

- A disregard for rules, laws, restraining orders, or boundaries of others.

- A lack of sincere accountability or insight into their behavior.

- An attitude of entitlement. They don't see a problem with stalking, hurting, or harassing you or others.

- Possessive, controlling, or jealous behavior. They may have made it clear through actions or words that you will always belong to them, or that they will hurt or kill whomever you date.

- You feel unsafe or fearful around them. They may have given you a look, or you are left with the feeling that they are "dark," "evil," "not human," or capable of murder.

Feelings of intimidation and fear are not normal emotions to experience in a relationship. They are a major warning sign that you need to take protective action immediately.

PART 2

UNDERSTANDING THE HOOKS THAT HAVE YOU

CHAPTER 11

THE 3 MAIN WAYS
MANIPULATION HAPPENS

Manipulation at any end of the spectrum tends to happen in three main ways: as a hit and run, hot and cold, or slow and steady. Understanding how each of these types of manipulation come across can help you to better see this behavior for what it is.

The hit-and-run. Some manipulators such as bullies, pickpockets, and emotional or physical abusers tend to have a hit-and-run approach. While each type of manipulation is different, the common ground is that this approach involves sudden and confusing behavior. The bully often uses the hit-and-run approach to get in a few well-placed comments that cut to the bone, in order to effectively knock their target down, or they become aggressive when something happens they don't like. Pickpockets and many scam artists looking for a fast way to get money use the hit-and-run approach. When they strike, they strike fast and hard, and leave the target reeling from what just happened. When an emotionally or physically abusive person uses the hit-and-run approach, it's either because they want to get their way or because they feel entitled to punish their target for some real or imagined transgression.

Some examples of the hit-and-run would be:

- A woman is on vacation abroad, where a good-looking man at a coffee shop approaches her. He flirts with her for half an hour, and then he says he has to leave. Shortly after, she goes to pay for her drink and realizes that her money and passport have been stolen out of her purse.

- A college student asks a question in class, and is told by the professor that his question is stupid, and something a child would ask.

- A pickpocket bumps into a woman on a train to distract her so he can steal her watch.

- A woman and her boyfriend are having dinner, when her boyfriend becomes argumentative over little things. No matter what she says, he shifts the argument to a new topic—it's as though he is trying to provoke a fight—which he is. He then breaks up with her. Over the next week she's spent numerous hours replaying that night, trying to figure out where things went off track and why. He contacts her that Monday, and is back to being the reasonable man she knows. Several months later she finds out from a stranger online that he had cheated on her while they were broken up. She confronts him, but in his mind he justifies it as they weren't dating.

Hot and cold. This is where everything may be fine one moment, and then suddenly things take a sharp turn. This is usually caused by the target disagreeing with the manipulator or behaving in a way that the manipulator disapproves of. If things take a sharp turn out of the blue, it may be because the manipulator is sadistic and therefore enjoys making the target uncomfortable simply because it's fun to watch them squirm.

Many abusive relationships fall into the hot-and-cold category. When it comes to dating, these types of manipulators begin relationships by heavily pursuing their love interest. However, if the objects of their desire act in any way that the manipulator doesn't approve of, their demeanor quickly becomes cold or cruel. When this happens, the target may think that if they could figure out what sets the manipulator off that they would be able to maintain peace in their relationship, but they are sadly mistaken. The line for what upsets the abuser is always shifting depending upon their mood. Neither of these things are predictable. What upset them one day won't another, and the result is that the target is continually uncertain and anxious about how to behave in fear of unintentionally setting them off.

Slow and steady. The slow-and-steady manipulators take their time building relationships and are often difficult to identify. The manipulators that move slow and steady are the ones with whom we tend to have ongoing contact within our lives—and they are ones that we may have the most trouble breaking free from. We may not even be aware that these people are manipulating us as their tactics may be cloaked in concern, or their problematic behavior has been ongoing long enough that we view it as normal.

When the slow-and-steady approach is used with the intention of exploiting a target for money, this is referred to as a "con" job. The term con is also very telling. It's short for "confidence" which is what these types of manipulators know they need to cultivate in order to better exploit the target down the road. Once confidence is established, a boundary is pushed (a request for money is made), confusion from the target ensues, more manipulation aimed at reassuring the target happens, exploitation occurs, the target is drained of their funds, and then discarded. If a con job like this is run under the guise of a serious relationship, the target is left both emotionally and financially devastated.

Keep in mind that because there is no one set type of manipulator, there is no one set game. The game is ever-changing based on what the manipulator thinks will work best on their target.

Some examples of the slow-and-steady approach:

Jane meets Thomas online. He tells her that he is in the military, and currently deployed overseas, but will return in a few weeks. Jane may not realize it, but subconsciously she may be placing more trust in Thomas than she realizes, as people generally trust those in the military, police, or helping professions. Thomas is handsome, charming, and quick to make her his whole world. And since Jane hasn't felt this loved or important in a very long time, she quickly makes Thomas her whole world as well. Soon, they are spending hours upon hours every day talking and texting.

When it comes time for Thomas to return to the US, he claims that he would like to get a hotel near her so that they could spend the next week together, and Jane agrees. Several days later, Thomas messages Jane telling her that there is a hold on his credit card, and he thinks it must be because he's been overseas for so long. Jane is hesitant to wire Thomas funds as she's heard about online scammers, but she is also eager to meet Thomas and to spend time together. Thomas promises to pay her back as soon as he's in town, and she believes this since he's in the military, seems so charming and sincere, and feels that she's in a serious relationship with him. She wires him $5,000, because, in her mind, she's not giving money to a stranger she's never met, *she's giving money to a man she feels is the love of her life and her soon-to-be husband.*

Over the next few weeks, Thomas messages her with one excuse after another as to why he's missed the plane and why he needs more money. Jane "loans" him a total of over $40,000 before Thomas quits returning her messages. Once she tells Thomas that she has no more money to lend him, Thomas stops messaging her. Reality comes crashing down on Jane as she realizes that she's been caught up in a scam.

Here is another common variation of the slow-and-steady approach and how it can set the stage for relationship problems later on in life:

Jackie was raised in a home with a difficult, demanding, and overbearing mother and a non-confrontational and avoidant father. Her mother had no respect for anyone else's time, energy, emotions, or boundaries, yet, she expected others to be there for her unconditionally and without question. If anyone were to challenge, question, or dare to say "no" to her, she'd fly into a rage, often accusing them of being selfish. Jackie learned at an early age that her mother's love was conditional and something that she needed to try and earn.

It took Jackie years of therapy for her to realize how her dynamic with her mother had bled over into other relationships in her life, leaving her with many hurtful or failed friendships and relationships as a result. Jackie realized that she didn't know how to give or receive love in healthy ways. She continually mistook being yelled at or controlled as proof that someone cared about her. If someone were to be kind and loving, she felt as though it was insincere. Jackie only felt comfortable in dynamics where she has to try and earn someone's love—which of course never happened and only left her with more pain.

Commonly-used phrases of the slow and steady:

No one understands me like you do.

I've done so much for you; I can't believe you are so selfish.

I need you.

A real friend would loan me money.

Family is forever. I can't believe you'd cut off contact with me.

You aren't perfect either; who are you to judge?

The commonalities between the different approaches are that all three come with confusion and a hook, whether or not that hook is seen for what it is. While the tactics, desired outcome, and level of self-awareness the manipulator has are all different; the driving force is the same: control over the target with the desire to win at all costs.

CHAPTER 12

SIGNS YOU ARE BEING MANIPULATED

If you are struggling to determine whether or not you are being manipulated, then hopefully this chapter will help to remove any lingering confusion.

Manipulators may:

- Threaten or imply that they will make your life difficult if you don't do what they want.

- Constantly threaten to end the relationship if you assert yourself, disagree with them, set a boundary, or don't give into their demands.

- Push for more, no matter how much you give, and act as if you are selfish or inconsiderate if you say no.

- Assume and expect that you will give in and label you as selfish, bad, greedy, unfeeling, manipulative, abusive, or uncaring when you don't.

- Regularly ignore or discount your feelings and wants.

- Make lavish promises contingent on your behavior and then rarely keep them.

- Shower you with approval or false promises when you give in to them and then take them away when you don't.

- Use money, fear, love, sex, guilt, or obligation as a weapon to get their way.

- They see no problem with cussing, yelling, cheating, lying, not paying you back, and so on, but would be outraged if you did the same to them.

- Have no respect for your boundaries, but insist that you respect theirs.

Signs You are in a Relationship with a Manipulative Person:

What I describe below is primarily in regards to a romantic relationship; however, some version of these dynamics is common with any manipulator.

- You can't tell if this person is wonderful or a total nightmare.

- You don't want to disagree or confront them out of fear they will make your life a living hell in some way.

- Your relationship with them can go from fine to confusing and complicated quickly, without your knowing why.

- You periodically feel picked on or provoked—like they are trying to insult you or start a fight.

- You can't seem to have an easy or enjoyable conversation with them with any degree of regularity. They seem to continually misunderstand what you say. With anyone else in your life, confusion like this could easily be cleared up with a short conversation, and you can't figure out why this isn't the case with them.

- You notice concerning personality changes within yourself.

- You become suspicious of their intentions and behavior, and wonder if they are being honest with you.

- They make subtle comments cloaked in concern that any issue you have with them is because you are jealous, paranoid, insecure, or losing your mind...and that you need help.

- You don't have this kind of complicated dynamic with others.

- They tell you that you have traits that no one (except other problematic people you've encountered) has ever accused you of before, such as being controlling, selfish, rude, impatient, jealous, needy, difficult, narcissistic, or abusive. What's confusing is that you feel these traits better describe their behavior rather than yours.

- They accuse you of lying, cheating, or stealing from them when you haven't.

- You hope that if you can please them enough that eventually you'll earn their respect, love, or even just decent treatment.

- You feel ground down and as though this relationship has really aged you.

- You feel defeated. Nothing that you do is ever good enough, and they continually point out something else about you that is "wrong."

- You are embarrassed or ashamed about how they treat you, and have left out major details such as verbal or physical abuse when talking to friends, family, or your therapist about problems in your relationship.

- You justify their mistreatment of you, but feel the final straw would be if they started treating your children the same way.

- You don't want to leave, because when things are good, they are really good.

- You are doing things against your morals or values to keep them happy.

- Their behavior never really changes; they just get better at hiding what they are doing.

- They make their issues of lying, cheating, stealing, or abusing you somehow your fault, and so you start working harder to fix this relationship.

- You are frustrated as to why you can't seem to get through to them that their behavior is a problem, and often wonder what it would really take.

- You don't trust your perception of events, and start turning towards others (usually the manipulator) to tell you what is and isn't a problem.

- You are fearful that the relationship issues are your fault, and that you somehow unknowingly sabotaged what could have been a wonderful relationship.

- You fear them living happily ever after with someone else—even though they were awful to you. If you do see pictures of them on social media with a new love interest, you see this as proof that you were in fact the problem and now someone else is getting to live your dream life with them.

Because so much confusion is present and ongoing rationalizations are given, it can be next to impossible to see a manipulative relationship for what it is while it's unfolding. So let me be clear: any one of the points listed above is a problem. None of this behavior is found in a healthy relationship.

CHAPTER 13

UNDERSTANDING TRAUMA BONDS

One of the most confusing and frustrating parts about manipulators is how and why they seem to have such a hold on their targets. Cult members will follow their leader to the bitter end, sex workers defend their pimps, and partners of abusive people keep going back. So why is this? There are multiple factors at work that contribute to making those on the receiving end feel so dependent upon, and addicted to, their manipulator. These trauma bonds are the result of seven different psychological and behavioral components: intermittent reinforcement, positive reinforcement, negative reinforcement, grooming, persistence, future faking, and Stockholm syndrome.

Trauma Bonding

Trauma bonding is a term that refers to the strong emotional attachment or bond of an abused person to their abuser. These bonds are forged through the emotional highs of lows of anxiety-inducing situations. Manipulators create tension when they want to get their way, for fun, or to punish their target. Any small act of perceived kindness from the manipulator is a relief, and that everything will be fine.

Because abusive people are generally not overtly or extremely abusive 100 percent of the time, the target clings to the moments of the good times as proof that everything is going to be okay. One way the target attempts to cope with all of the mental anguish that their partner's bad behavior brings is to shift their thinking from "me" to "we." This way, the stress (abuse) in the dynamic isn't something that happens to them alone. Instead, it is a shared experience that they survive together. The target feels that they and the abusive person are "going through so much together," *instead of seeing it as being put through so much by this person.*

This new mindset is often fed by the manipulator who may claim that "going through so much" together is what commitment is all about, and that it makes a relationship stronger. Of course, this expectation and understanding is only how the abuser views their behavior. If the target were to treat the abuser the same way, they would have left. Because of the abuser's inability to see themselves as anything other than right, if the target wants out, the abuser is outraged and will exclaim that the target is the one who isn't invested in the relationship. Never mind that the target is leaving because the manipulator has been the one with no shortage of relationship-destroying behavior.

If a target buys into the manipulation, a deeper, more dysfunctional bond is created, as now there are three people in the relationship: the Mr. Hyde side of the abuser, the target, and the Dr. Jekyll side of the abuser. The problem is that there really is no third person; the abusive person and both sides of their behavior are one and the same. If the target doesn't realize they are in an abusive relationship, they may go to great lengths to appease the abuser in an effort to keep the relationship going. The reason is that the target feels addicted to the abuser, and is desperate to make this relationship work. The thought process is that while the abuser is the one who causes the pain, only the abuser can take it away. So while this relationship is destroying them, they can't imagine living without it. What's sad is that so many of us have confused these intense cravings or unhinged neediness for love. They aren't. *They are the result of trauma bonds.* Love doesn't hurt, and it doesn't destroy, and it doesn't require that you sacrifice your dignity or self-respect for it.

When the target starts confusing abuse for love, they are sent on an emotional roller coaster ride through hell. The low times are full of stress and fear of their partner hurting or leaving them. When stress and fear are present, cortisol and the chemicals that compose adrenaline (norepinephrine and epinephrine) are released. The result is chronic feelings of anxiety, which lead to feelings of desperation to make things work, and an unhinged neediness. These feelings are deactivated or calmed by the pressure being taken off and things returning to some degree of normal. When the target has the reassurance that the relationship will continue, they get a rush of dopamine, which is a "feel good" chemical and oxytocin which is a chemical that facilitates both attachment and bonding.

These extreme ups and downs, coupled with any abandonment issues the target may have, create extreme cravings and dependency. When this manipulationship ends, the target may feel addicted to this abusive person and wonder what is wrong with them for still missing or "loving" them. Additionally, any relationship that the target has after this that doesn't involve highs and lows can feel numb or flat. If the target is not aware that they were abused (which is often the case if they weren't beaten repeatedly) they may struggle with wondering if the ending of the relationship was their fault or if they lost their soulmate. And they may worry that they'll never feel this way about anyone again. Because of the intensity of the trauma bonds, the target may also leave this relationship, but then unbeknownst to them, be primed for abuse if they are still confusing these intense, soul-crushing feelings for love, and drawn to new relationships that feel the same.

Intermittent Reinforcement

There are two main ways that behavior is shaped: through continuous reinforcement or through intermittent reinforcement. Continuous reinforcement is when behavior is reinforced, meaning, rewarded or punished, in a continuous or predictable way. For example, if you are toilet training a young child, and every time he uses the toilet you lavish praise on him, the child learns to associate that going to the bathroom is a good thing and makes mom or dad happy. You are shaping the child's behavior by continually reinforcing that using the toilet is a good thing. When expectations and outcomes are clearly understood, we know what is expected of us. This level of predictability allows for a feeling of safety and comfort for those on the receiving end of this.

Intermittent reinforcement is when behavior is rewarded or punished in an erratic way. Let's take the same example of toilet training a child. If you were to act in an unpredictable way, such as congratulate your child some of the time he used the toilet and completely ignore him other times, or if you were to yell at him to hurry up, the child is going to struggle connecting what he needs to do in order to get your approval and stay out of trouble.

The result of unpredictable reward and punishment, or intermittently reinforced behavior, is anxiety, depression, and feelings of hopelessness and helplessness, because their actions may or may not lead them to the desired outcome. When a person is on the receiving end of having their behavior intermittently reinforced, at first, they often double up their efforts to appease the other person in an attempt to get the tension, icy presence, ignoring, or abuse to stop. However, if this doesn't work, the target tends to give up and may become quiet and withdrawn around the person who is impossible to please.

For example, let's say Chloe has an overbearing and critical mother. In order to avoid being belittled or berated, Chloe always makes sure that she looks and acts in a way that her mother would approve. However, there was never any guarantee. One day her mother would approve of her outfit or her friends, but then a week later she wouldn't. All of her mother's unpredictable behavior left Chloe feeling continually anxious and insecure in general, but especially around her mother.

Being on the receiving end of intermittent reinforcement isn't just frustrating, it's corrosive to a person's individuality and emotional health. *Additionally, it can also create an addictive response in the person who is trying to gain their desired outcome.* The reason for this addictive response is that there is a rush of a feel good hormone called dopamine that comes from achieving the reward. This rush of dopamine isn't found in continuous reinforcement, because everything is predictable. When we put a lot of time and effort into something, and when we repeatedly fail along the way, success is that much more rewarding. The same is true with being able to please a difficult partner. The stress created by the emotional lows can make the relief of the highs addictive. In certain situations, having our hard work rewarded can be beneficial, but in terms of trying to please a person with difficult, demanding, and erratic behavior, it can lead to all kinds of problems.

When toxic relationships like this end, the former target is often left feeling like their chemistry with others is "flat" or completely lacking. This is because healthy relationships are predictable and aren't an emotional roller coaster full of intensity or the hard work required to earn being treated with kindness.

If a person has grown up in a home where attention and affection wasn't predictably given, then having to earn it from a partner later on in life might not feel problematic. In fact, it might feel comfortable and any relationship where love, respect, and good treatment are freely given might feel inauthentic or anxiety-inducing, because if they didn't earn it, then this also means they could easily lose it.

Positive Reinforcement

Positive reinforcement is a type of continuous reinforcement: when a person acts in a desired way, that behavior is rewarded positively on a reliable basis. For example, a boss who notices when his employees are doing a good job and lets them know how appreciated they are.

However, positive reinforcement can be one of the many tools a manipulator uses by rewarding their target in a positive way for their submission. For example, the manipulator may shower the target with attention and affection for doing things their way. The target learns that if they give in, then they'll either avoid being abused or get some crumbs of kindness thrown their way.

Negative Reinforcement

Negative reinforcement is the other type of continuous reinforcement, as it provides reliable punishment for behavior that is deemed problematic. In the case of abuse, the negative reinforcement may be nagging, yelling, put downs, the silent treatment, or threatening consequences if the target doesn't behave in a certain way.

People reinforced in this way tend to become angry, resentful, ground down, disempowered, develop low self-esteem, and are afraid to try new things or new approaches to a problem. When a person internalizes their mistakes, and thinks that they are incompetent or incapable or is continually unable to get their needs met no matter how hard they try, they develop what's called "learned helplessness." They feel they cannot do anything right and have no control to affect change, so they stop trying. They tend to internalize their mistakes and see themselves as deeply flawed instead of seeing a mistake for what it is. Or, if they've been around a manipulator long enough, they might see themselves as bad, wrong, and deeply flawed, instead of realizing this is only the manipulator's pathological view of them, and isn't reality. This is often the case with children who grow up being the targets of abuse.

Grooming

Grooming is when manipulators shape or "groom" their target's behavior into what they want. This grooming may be done through acts of kindness or threats of punishment. The manipulator's actions can be done using intermittent, continuous, positive, or negative reinforcement, or grooming may occur with severe one-time consequences. For example, many child predators groom their targets with gifts, attention, and special treatment that leaves the child feeling as though this predator is a friend. With severe one-time consequences, the target learns quickly, often with one incident, to never do whatever they did again. For example, the target might have worn lipstick and the manipulator began accusing them of wearing makeup because they were cheating. In an effort to reassure their partner, the target may stop wearing lipstick. Grooming can either be done in overt, covert, passive-aggressive or aggressive ways, with the implied message ranging from, "Act like this or else I'll pull away my attention or affection," or "Act like this or else you'll have hell to pay."

Persistence

Many targets of manipulators, as well as those around them, confuse their persistence with sincerity. After all, most people don't go to great lengths to win back their partner, or make their marriage work if they don't really mean it. However, manipulators will. Make no mistake--persistence doesn't always mean a person is sincere. If someone is trying to guilt you into forgiving them or won't leave you alone after you've told them to, then this behavior is about control, and shows a lack of respect for your boundaries.

Future Faking

Future faking is when the promise of the ultimate prize (the hook) the target desires is dangled in front of them. The manipulator might talk about getting married, having a baby, getting sober, getting into therapy, doing whatever it takes to make the relationship work, or, if they are an employer, giving a raise or a promotion.

Future faking fuels a fantasy with talk of the target's ideal future. Down the road, once the emotional roller coaster starts, they may make promises to change, shows signs of remorse, and bring up the target's ideal future as a way to persuade them into giving the manipulator another chance. Because future faking involves the manipulator saying what the target needs to hear, this talk (or short-lived actions) are often confused with the relationship turning a positive corner and getting back on track. Future faking doesn't just lead to disappointment, it leads to profound amounts of psychological and emotional damage. The reason is that the manipulator often places some of the blame for their bad behavior onto the target. The result is that now the target is working overtime to smooth out issues within the relationship that weren't theirs to begin with. All of the target's work results in them trying to be a better communicator, a better spouse, better in bed, and somehow less of a problem. The result is they've become more submissive, taken on inappropriate levels of responsibility for their partner's behavior, and have silenced even more parts of themselves, all so the relationship can work.

However, much like chasing a mirage in the desert, the ideal future never comes. Instead, the targets wear themselves out only to get more abuse in return. It often takes years for a target to get to the point where they are so exhausted and frustrated with nothing changing, that they start to see this future faking as the empty talk that it is. At this point, tremendous guilt, shame, embarrassment, and rage for not seeing things clearly often set in.

Stockholm Syndrome

The psychological term "Stockholm Syndrome" was coined by the criminologist and psychiatrist Nils Bejerot in 1973 after he assisted the police during a bank robbery in Stockholm, Sweden where four employees (three women and one man) were held hostage for six days.

During their captivity, it was noted that the hostages developed strong emotional attachments to their captors, which they claimed stemmed from their captors showing them kindness in the midst of their captivity. These small acts of kindness seemed to negate the fact that their lives had been threatened. Several months after being released, it was discovered that some of the hostages were still viewing their captors in a positive light. One woman even had the captors over for dinner once they were out of prison.

Psychologists wanted to know if the Stockholm Bank incident was a unique occurrence, or if it was more common than originally thought. Since then, studies have revealed that those being abused formed trauma bonds with their abuser as a result of a variety of stressful and abusive situations. These bonds are strengthened due to the mix of tension and relief that accompanies intermittent reinforcement.

Understanding What Has You Hooked

Once you have clarity about the hook that has you, you can then work toward developing a plan. Even if you aren't ready to work on developing a plan, having the awareness of what's driving you to hold on can help you begin to see your thoughts and responses to them much more clearly. Understanding what has you hooked can be really insightful, and can sometimes be the clarity that sets a person free.

However, it's important to understand that change of any kind is always difficult--no matter how needed it is or how ready you are.

In addition to any trauma bonds that may be present, take some time to examine what other emotional hooks have you caught up in this dynamic. A good start to getting this clarity is to ask yourself the following questions:

- Are you staying in this dynamic because you are lonely, or intimidated by the thought of being alone?

- Are you keeping this person in your life because they are family, and you feel obligated to keep in regular contact or to keep trying to make the relationship work?

- Are you holding onto hope that if you continue to stick around that you will eventually get whatever it is that they've been promising? (For example, a promotion, to get married, to get sober, etc.)

- Have you given money, and hope by being nice you will eventually get repaid?

- Are you thinking that things will change if you keep trying to get through to them...even though you've been trying for months, years, or decades?

- Are you concerned that if you leave, they will find someone else, and that new person will reap all of the benefits of your attempts to change them?

- Are you intimidated by the thought of confronting them, and that doing so will only make things worse?

- Are you afraid that confronting them will hurt them emotionally?

- Are you afraid of letting go and the sadness and potential emotional or financial loss associated with it?
- Are you ready to let go, but just don't know how to end it?
- Have you already experienced a lot of loss in your life and don't want to go through another one?

One of the biggest changes you will have to make is in letting go of the hope-fueled fantasy that someday you will have this fulfilling relationship with them when none of their actions point to this being a possibility. Seeing your fantasy for what it is can be incredibly hard, and often involves grieving the loss of the relationship you thought you had or the relationship you thought was possible...but giving up this fantasy is the beginning of setting yourself free.

CHAPTER 14

THE PROGRESSION
OF MANIPULATION

Manipulation is progressive, corrosive, and the early warning sign of more severe verbal, emotional, psychological, sexual, financial, or spiritual abuse to come. Manipulation, like cancer, can be difficult to see in the early stages. Additionally, with both, there is a progression of symptoms if we know what to look for. The progression of manipulation can be broken down into ten different stages. Since every manipulator and dynamic are different, the order, degree, and frequency of these stages will vary.

The ten stages are:
1. Confidence is established.
2. An emotional bond is established.
3. The target receives a boundary push.
4. Confusion from the target occurs.
5. An emotional hook is dropped.

6. The target resists.

7. The manipulator applies pressure.

8. The target is threatened.

9. The target complies.

10. The dynamic worsens or it ends.

Here are these steps in more detail:

1. Some degree of confidence is established.

In order for confidence to be established, some degree of trust must be present. Master manipulators do an excellent job of establishing trust quickly by saying all the right things and even backing up what they are saying with all of the right actions. Because they are able to act the part long enough for a target's trust to deepen into confidence, targets are quick to gloss over red flags once they do begin to arise. A manipulator's ability to establish and exploit another is why they are referred to as a con artist, which is the shortened term for confidence artist. The more confidence that is established, the more damaging and longer-lasting the manipulation will be. Many scam artists, child predators, and human traffickers rely heavily on cultivating confidence both with their target and those around them.

2. An emotional bond is established.

Emotional bonds are strengthened by the amount of time the target spends with the manipulator--either in person or online. These bonds are often cultivated through the exchange of personal experiences, spending significant amounts of time together, sexual intimacy, or the manipulator continually reassuring the target that they can be trusted and for them to share all of their hopes and fears with them.

3. The target receives a boundary push.

Manipulators push limits to get what they want or simply because they feel entitled to treat others poorly. A boundary push is some sort of request or action with which the target has an issue. While other people may not know where our boundaries are unless we make them known, the boundary pushes of a manipulator are often inappropriate, and cross a line that any reasonable adult would know not to cross.

This is where the vast majority of targets get tripped up—especially those who have been in an abusive relationship before. *If you struggle with identifying when you are being treated in a way that you don't like or when someone has crossed your boundary, this is a problem that needs to be addressed. It's really hard to hold the line if you don't know where the line is.*

If the target gives into the boundary push, the manipulator has now set the pace and those boundary pushes will become more frequent and more severe. The longer this continues, your wants, needs, thoughts, and opinions will become less of a priority until there is no sense of you left. Even if the initial boundary push starts off small, if left unaddressed it will grow with time as the manipulator becomes bolder.

Some examples of common boundary pushes early on include someone:

- Calling you pet names when you've just met them
- Talking about sex or asking for sexy pictures from you when you hardly know them
- Making inappropriate requests, such wanting to borrow money, move in, borrow your car, etc.
- Cussing or yelling at you
- Intimidating behavior of any kind (threats, hints of threats, throwing, punching, or breaking things)
- Wanting to talk or touch you more than you are comfortable with

4. Some degree of confusion is experienced by the target.

Out of all the signs experienced, confusion is the one that is the most significant if we can take it seriously as the major warning sign that it is. *Confusion is often the first sign of a problem.* When a person is being manipulated by someone they have a relationship with, they experience confusion and then they rationalize it. *The reason for this is that they are experiencing problematic behavior, but wish that they weren't.* The deeper the relationship, the deeper the denial.

For example, we might experience a flash of confusion when our partner is being overly secretive with their phone and who they are texting, if someone is walking faster than normal behind us when we are in a parking garage, or if our boss has an inappropriate request. Any one of these scenarios tends to register as a "huh, that's weird." However, it's the situations that we are invested in that we have the hardest time seeing clearly and taking action on. It can be difficult addressing issues at work or home when doing so might risk our employment or our relationship.

5. An emotional hook is dropped.

Emotional hooks come in different forms, although most of them involve fear, obligation, guilt, sympathy, hope, or love, and the most effective hooks are directed at a target's vulnerabilities. These hooks might be something that is more concrete and positive, such as a promotion, a promise to get married, to get sober, or to stop being abusive. Or the hook might be sympathy-inducing, which is often the case with various internet scams, or manipulators claim to be ill, suicidal, or helpless without you.

If the hook is emotional, it might appeal to the target's low self-esteem, loneliness, or desire to be loved. If the hook involves fear, intimidation may be involved, such as threatening to withhold child support, ruining your career, or hurting someone you care about. Another type of hook that involves fear is if the manipulator threatens to end the relationship if you don't do what they want. Regardless of the emotional hook, the dynamic has now become unequal, and the target is most likely in a scramble to either make things work or get things back to some degree of being tolerable.

6. The target resists.

After the boundary is pushed, the target may initially put up a mild protest or avoid the manipulator to keep the situation from escalating. This is frequently the case if the target doesn't like confrontation or only knows how to navigate uncomfortable situations by being nice. When a target is so "go with the flow," they don't realize that going along with others in order to get along with them is a problem.

It's at this stage where the target's confusion and mental anguish begin to increase. Pressure from the manipulator creates tension, and the target, feeling no choice but to give in, winds up doing so—often mistaking these boundary violations and their subsequent caving in for appropriate compromise that all people make when they are in a committed relationship. If this pressure, tension, and resentment is ongoing, the target will begin to feel that this relationship is difficult and confusing, but may not know why. They may think they are making a big deal out of nothing. Once the target sees manipulation for what it is, this mindset of compliance will be replaced with resentment, and eventually anger at not seeing this clearly before.

7. The manipulator applies pressure.

This is where the manipulator continues to push for their desired outcome until the target completely drops their boundaries. At first it may appear that there is no pressure present, and that the manipulator wants to talk over the issue. However, the conversation will quickly devolve into a lecture or accusations that the target is mean, controlling, manipulative, or unreasonable when in reality the target is only trying to assert themselves. These accusations are used as a form of pressure on the target to cave. If pressuring the target doesn't work, the manipulator may pepper in charm or reassurance followed by pleading.

The manipulator may say something like:

I thought you loved me.

If you loved me/wanted this job/were a friend you would do this.

I would never lie to you or hurt you.

At this point, fear, obligation, guilt, and sympathy are being laid on thick, and the target may become confused as to whether or not their boundaries are reasonable, or wonder if they are the difficult one. This type of introspection can be ongoing when a manipulator is present. *Each time we buy into thinking our boundaries, feelings, or opinions are the problem, we are replacing our reality with the manipulator's.*

8. The target is threatened.

If the target doesn't cave into the manipulator's demands, the manipulator will raise the stakes. At this point, direct or indirect threats involving emotional or physical pain or unhappiness are made. The manipulator may manufacture undeserved guilt within the target by accusing them of being uncaring, cruel, or a bad parent. They may also make threats such as ending the relationship, talking about suicide, telling the target they should die or kill themselves, or that they will kill the target. If the manipulator does lash out, they will blame the target for provoking them, when in reality, all the target did was set boundaries.

9. The target complies.

In an effort to prevent the manipulator from escalating further and actually following through on any of their threats, as well as to release some of the anxiety and tension that the manipulator's threats cause, the target gives in. When the manipulator gets their way, the immediate pressure has been removed from the target, often leaving them to think that things have turned a corner, and that this relationship can be salvaged.

However, this sense of relief and period of calm are often short-lived. The reality is that with each concession, the target is losing touch with their boundaries, identity, and self-esteem, while the manipulator has gained more ground and the relationship is continuing to become more unbalanced. While things may appear calm, they are actually significantly worse as now the manipulator knows what buttons to push and to what extent they need to escalate their bad behavior in order to get the target to comply from here on out. *The groundwork is now set for a pattern of demands and pressure, and the cycle of manipulation worsens.*

10. The dynamic worsens or it ends.

At this point, one of three things will most likely happen:

- **The target doesn't comply, and instead holds their boundary.** If the target starts holding their boundary, they are hopefully aware of the different buttons the manipulator has been pushing so they can hold their ground on all fronts. Additionally, when they go to hold their ground, it's vital that they do so in a safe way. Setting boundaries with a person that has been dangerous, or that you fear might become that way, is only a good idea if you are doing so from afar and in the most self-protective way possible.

- **The manipulator spots another target and moves on.** When a manipulator moves on, it's usually for one of two reasons: the target stops giving in, or the manipulator becomes excited by a fresh, new prospect. If the manipulator moves on, the target may struggle with feeling responsible for not doing more to keep the relationship intact. It's important to realize that the target can give and give, and do everything the manipulator wants, and put up with all kinds of lying, cheating, stealing, and abuse, and still "lose" the relationship. There isn't enough a target can do to "earn" their love, because a connection with a pathological manipulator will only ever be a one-way street—and real love can't be earned anyway.

  Regardless of the reason the manipulator moves on, this doesn't mean they will necessarily leave the former target alone. In terms of a romantic relationships, it's extremely common for a manipulator to date or even marry someone else, but continue to message the former target with professions of their love or to threaten to harm the target if the target were to date someone else. Remember, their game is all about control and winning. If they become possessive or threatening, this isn't romantic or a sick sign that they care. If you are in this position, keep your emotional shields up and your boundaries strong...and consider moving as far away as you can from them.

The target is left wondering how the manipulator can move on so quickly, like they never existed, and how they seem so indifferent and unaffected. They are left nursing the pain of profound heartbreak, while simultaneously struggling with confusion about why the manipulator left and what they could have done differently. They may be in a state of shock and grief, desperate for answers and for the manipulator to return. It's not uncommon for the manipulator to resurface, claiming that they care or that they want to be "friends" with the target. The target may have mixed feelings of hesitation and longing and agree to this "friendship" as a way to keep the manipulator in their life.

What they don't realize is that the manipulator isn't looking to be their friend; the manipulator is looking to keep them on the hook to use them for whatever they might need: a place to stay, money, sex, or social contacts. Or, if the manipulator is sadistic, they may call or text the former target and want to tell them all about their most recent date, or how happy they are with their new partner. If the target gets upset by this, the manipulator yet again blames the target for not being supportive or wanting to see them happy. Any of these ploys are to keep the target strung along, keeping their hope alive, and preventing them from moving forward. If this describes what you are going through, please know that you aren't being petty or holding a grudge if you don't want to be friends with an ex. It's perfectly fine to cut off communication with someone who has treated you poorly.

At this point, the target is most likely unaware that their relationship was an abusive one--especially if there was no verbal or physical abuse. However, a manipulative relationship is an abusive relationship, and psychological and emotional abuse can take many targets years or decades to understand what happened as well as to see the damage that's been done. Down the road, the target may begin to question how they got caught up with someone like this, and how they allowed themselves to be so mistreated and didn't realize it at the time.

As they are seeking clarity, the target is simultaneously struggling with feeling fearful of how they can keep themselves safe from the manipulator and others in the future. Shame, guilt, embarrassment, distrust of others, and struggling with getting validation or support often follow as they reach out to others for support, and instead get blamed for being manipulated and abused or are pressured to "get over it and move on." This added blame only further serves to create more feelings of embarrassment, shame, and worthlessness.

Now the target is even more vulnerable and the risk of them returning to the manipulator or getting involved with another one is very high. However, it doesn't have to be this way. Parts four and five of this book will help you gain the strategies and insights needed in order to break free from manipulation once and for all.

- **The target caves in.** When the target caves in, they usually do so either out of hope or fear. They cave in because they want the relationship to continue or they cave because they are afraid of what will happen if they don't. Regardless of the reason, this dynamic is now at a new low. If the target continues to cave in and stay, they will stay until things become so painful they cannot stay any longer. At this point, it will take every ounce of strength they have to leave the dynamic. If the manipulator still leaves, the target may be so devastated that they end their life.

CHAPTER 15

THE PSYCHOLOGICAL PROGRESSION OF THE TARGET

While manipulation is progressive, so is the target's response to it. The emotional and psychological progression that a target experiences is confusion, introspection, rationalization, and erosion.

Here's what this progression looks like in motion:

Confusion: The target experiences problematic behavior and doesn't understand why. Confusion ensues, and they begin looking for reasons as to why things have become tense or overly-complicated, or why the manipulator is being so cold, cruel, or callous.

Introspection: In an attempt to understand why the manipulator is so upset, the target finds themselves replaying any and all interactions that led up to the manipulator's icy behavior. Going through these various encounters with a fine-tooth comb, the target continually wonders what they did that was so wrong and if they are the difficult one, or if the manipulator is over-reacting or maybe even being abusive. It often takes targets (and most people in general) a very long time before they identify abusive behavior as abuse. At best, they may have only dipped their toe into that idea, because calling abusive behavior abuse can seem like an over-reaction— especially when society is quick to minimize and make excuses for it.

Rationalization: The target is now at a crossroads: do they stay or do they go? If they decide to stay, it's usually because they want or need for this dynamic to continue. If they do not see this manipulative and crazy-making behavior for what it is, they will begin to justify their mistreatment. The result is that, over time, they are unknowingly replacing their reality and sense of self with the pathologically skewed perceptions of the manipulator. The whole time this is happening, the target is thinking that they are doing the right thing by changing the things about themselves that the manipulator deems as problematic in an attempt to make the relationship work.

The target rationalizes their mistreatment through minimization, justification, and denial. They may tell themselves that they must have misinterpreted what the manipulator said or did, that they have unresolved issues from their past, that they are too sensitive, or that the manipulator had a bad day or a bad childhood and can't help the way they behave. Or worse, they accept responsibility and blame for their mistreatment, thinking that the manipulator is right, and that if they just behaved differently the manipulator wouldn't yell, give the silent treatment, cuss, threaten, hit, and so on.

164

If the target believes that if they act the way the manipulator wants that things will eventually get better and that they will be treated fairly or decently, they are mistaken. Instead, a complete erosion of who they are is in motion as the manipulator now controls their thoughts, feelings, and behavior.

Erosion: The comparison with Alice in Wonderland is often used to describe the upside-down reality that results from being in a relationship with a pathologically manipulative person. It's a lot like how Alice felt at the Mad Hatter's tea party with being told that everything she ever knew about herself or the world around her was wrong. What was once up is now down, and what is down is up.

Here are some of the critical pieces of a person's sense of self that are often eroded and how it happens:

- The ability to identify a problem is diminished, because every time the target had a problem with the manipulator's behavior they were told that they were the one with the problem.

- Self-esteem is diminished when the abuser continually insults or degrades them—especially if the target comes to believe all of these horrible things about them are true.

- The ability to be self-protective is diminished because the target was told that their boundaries weren't reasonable or needed. Now, the target struggles with wondering if any issue they have with someone's behavior is unreasonable. This leads the target to struggle being able to identify when they are mistreated and what to do about it.

- The ability to trust others is diminished, because they once trusted someone who profoundly hurt them.

- The ability to make decisions is diminished, because they've continually been told that every decision they've made that wasn't in line with the manipulator's thinking was wrong.

Some examples of how reality becomes eroded:

I didn't say that we'd go out this weekend, and you are crazy for ever thinking that I did. Oh you have text messages proving what I said? Well, you must have faked them.

I know I cheated multiple times, but how can you give up on us so quickly? Don't you love me?

I had to open up credit cards in your name because my credit is terrible. You are selfish for having a problem with this after I've done so much for you over the years.

I can't believe you are pressing charges against me for hitting you. It only happened that once; you are making a big deal out of nothing.

Because this level of manipulation has gradually become the target's new normal, the target doesn't realize how profound the damage being done to their thinking, identity, or self-esteem really is until they leave. Once they do realize it, they are overwhelmed by the monumental task of untangling the manipulator's pathologically skewed version of them from who they actually are. *Attempting to sort all of this out is incredibly difficult since the target has been programmed to doubt their every thought, to automatically assume that they are wrong, and to look to the manipulator to tell them how to think and act.* Once the manipulator is gone, the target often feels lost and struggles to get back in touch with what they really think and feel.

While a former target must learn how to validate themselves, in the beginning they will most likely need to find that "self" before they can begin to validate it. When a person is struggling with trying to sort out harmful advice and behavior from the helpful, it can be extremely confusing. There is no shortage of dysfunctional thinking out there.

If you are in need of some help, a trusted long-time friend or family member, therapist, or life coach who are empowering and have a healthy understanding of what boundaries, abuse, and manipulation are can help. However, finding these people can sometimes be a challenge. If this is the case, then joining a support group can be profoundly helpful. I have two different online groups that are both free. One is for people who are focused on understanding manipulation and abuse, and the other group is for people who have gained that clarity and who are now ready to focus solely on their healing. You can find out more about both groups by going to my website: www.thriveafterabuse.com

CHAPTER 16

SEVEN POINTS TO CONSIDER BEFORE STARTING COUPLE'S COUNSELING

It's not uncommon for a manipulator to suggest that the two of you repair the relationship in therapy. However, going to therapy with a manipulative or otherwise emotionally immature person will often make things worse. If you are considering therapy with a manipulative person, be aware of these important points. While the seven points below pertain to couple's counseling, these same issues can surface in any type of counseling a manipulator enters, whether it be family, individual, spiritual, or court-appointed counseling. Because they are so manipulative and have such a pathological world view, it's common for them to return from counseling saying that their therapist thinks that *you* are a narcissist, manipulative, or abusive.

Here are seven additional points to consider:

1. They may suggest therapy because they think *you* are the one who needs to change.

Most of the time manipulators don't have the self-awareness to know that their behavior is a problem. If they suggest therapy, they may be doing so because they think that you are the one who needs to change. If a person lacks emotional maturity, then odds are they also lack sincere accountability, feel justified in their behavior, and have no understanding or respect for the boundaries of other people. Before you even start therapy, it's a good idea to get clear on what kind of changes you need to see and in what time frame so that you get a clear idea of how much time, energy, and money you are willing to put towards seeing if they will change.

2. Going to therapy may only be another level to their game.

If you have a manipulator in your life who is more on the exploitative, charming, and schmoozing side of the spectrum, they may do a great job of pretending to be accountable for their behavior. They may apologize profusely, sob uncontrollably, make grand displays of how sorry they are, or appear to be sincere, remorseful, accountable, and dedicated to making this relationship work in front of the counselor.

None of this means anything unless their behavior actually changes. And more often than not, when they make these grand public displays of apology, it has nothing to do with them being sincere; it's all about them getting their ego boosted by others thinking they are so amazing, caring, insightful, and an overall wonderful human being. So keep this in mind. There's a saying that goes, "If you want to feed the homeless, feed the homeless. If you want to let the world know how wonderful you are for feeding the homeless, then you are feeding your ego." Manipulators are notorious for these kinds of over-the-top displays of goodness. However, some are significantly more subtle with their displays of goodness or sincerity, but the displays are all for show nonetheless. I've worked with targets who were outraged and confused as to how their ex could march in a domestic violence awareness parade while their ex continued to stalk and send them verbally abusive text messages. I've worked with targets who had their spouse go crying to their spiritual leader begging to help them save their marriage while they were cheating the whole time.

3. True change takes time, and no matter how much therapy, rehab, religion, or love a person gets, there is no guarantee they will actually change.

True change is hard work and a process—it's not an event. Change rarely happens within three therapy sessions—and there's a very solid chance it won't happen within thirty, *if it ever happens at all.* A person can go to therapy for decades and not change enough for the relationship to work. When this happens, it's because they may not be ready to change; they may not be a good fit with their therapist; they may be working on other issues; they may have a skewed perception of their behavior and the therapist isn't getting an accurate view of what's really going on; or, they aren't interested in changing.

If they truly aren't interested in changing, but are going to therapy, it could be because they are court-appointed to be there, they have to meet with a social worker/case manager to get certain services from the government. Or, perhaps, they are going to therapy and consciously lying to the therapist so they can create a paper trail of their good behavior, or to get the therapist's testimony in the future; or, maybe because it's fun for them to see what they can get a mental health clinician to believe. If they are sadistic, they may simply be going to therapy because they want an audience to listen to all of their heinous behavior just so they can watch the therapist squirm.

4. They may seem to suddenly have insight, appear sincere and remorseful, and act the part of a changed person.

If on the first few sessions they go from having no moral compass to being an honest, loving, attentive, loyal partner who is full of insight and able to communicate effectively, then odds are they are putting on a show. You may find yourself scratching your head wondering how and why they were chronically cheating and lying for years when a few honest conversations could have kept your marriage together. This is especially true if they seem to have no problem being open and honest in therapy. If someone with this level of pathological behavior claims to have been able to self-reflect, promises never to do it again (maybe even offer to take a lie detector test to prove it), and overall transforms into your ideal partner, then there is a solid chance they are acting the part of changing and are better at hiding what they are doing.

5. Be on the lookout for subtle blame-shifting and manipulation.

If they seem to be fully accountable for their behavior, but then say that the reason they cheated, lied, hit, or whatnot was because of something you did, then they aren't being accountable for their behavior. This subtle sleight of hand can be tricky to spot. They may say that they cheated because they didn't feel comfortable bringing up issues about the relationship, or that they cheated because you worked too much or that you gained weight. If you or the therapist don't see the blame shifting for what it is, you may leave the session thinking how wonderful therapy seems to be working and how happy you are to know what you need to fix. See what happened there? You and the therapist have both been roped into their manipulation that in order for them to have a moral compass you need to behave a certain way. Don't fall for this, and, also, please understand that therapists are human too. They don't know and see everything, and they aren't an expert on your life—you are. If there is some truth to the issues the manipulator brings up, then keep those separate; don't let them off the hook. You may have been working too much or gained weight, but that doesn't make their cheating okay. If you do want to work on some of the issues they brought up, that's fine; however, they still need to own their part.

6. What you say in therapy may be used against you.

Before you start therapy with them, it's important that some ground rules are established, and that these rules apply to both of you.

Some rules to consider would be that what is said in therapy can't be used against the other person, and that no verbal or emotional abuse is to happen during a therapy session.

A skilled therapist isn't going to allow anyone to be re-victimized or abused during couple's counseling. If this happens, it should be addressed immediately and directly and made clear that it is not to happen again. If you continue to be abused or re-victimized in therapy, and the therapist doesn't end the session, it's okay to leave. It's also okay to talk to your therapist one-on-one about this, or to get a new therapist. If your partner is flat-out lying, trying to manipulate the therapist by playing the victim, or being verbally abusive or attempting to gaslight you during a session, it's okay to say that you want to talk to the therapist alone, that you want to stop the session, or even that you want to stop couple's counseling altogether.

If you get into couple's counseling and what you say in there is later used to shame, belittle, or insult you in any way, shape or form, this is abusive, and not okay. Their actions have now made it clear that they are not an emotionally safe person, and you would be wise to go into self-protection mode and not reveal anything deeply personal until they've proven with time and action that they can be trusted. If you want to continue couple's therapy, then it would be a good idea to let the therapist know what happened.

Because manipulators will most likely spin these rules to make them work best for them, let me clarify a bit. For example, let's say they share during therapy that they have had an affair. Once you are made aware of this, you decide you want a divorce. They may claim that you are using what they said against them by wanting a divorce. This is not the case. You are making a self-protective decision based upon information they provided. An example of information used against the other person would be along the lines of your saying that your father left when you were a child, and then during your next fight, they bring that information into play saying that it's no wonder your father left because you are intolerable. Comments like these are designed to cut deep, and that's not okay.

Additionally, manipulators may use sensitive information you shared against you and then apologize for doing so. Even if they apologize, that doesn't make their behavior okay as there is still damage done. This is along the lines of someone saying, "I don't mean to be rude, but..." and then ending their statement with a rude comment. Just because they initially said that they didn't mean to be rude, doesn't make their rudeness somehow less hurtful or okay. Passive-aggressive digs like this are just as hurtful as aggressive ones, and are not okay.

7. Realize they are *not* going to give the same account of events as you.

No two people recall events in the same way. This is especially true if one of those people continually denies, minimizes, and justifies their behavior. Not only has this person lacked accountability for their actions, *they've rewritten reality to make everyone else at fault.* These mental gymnastics are how and why most manipulators don't think they are being manipulative.

175

Even for the most skilled therapist, it might take a while to see a more accurate picture of what's really going on, if they ever do, especially if the manipulator is in individual therapy and the therapist has no other perspective of events other than what they are being told.

Let's say, for example, that they did something you would consider undeniable, such as they hit you and then threw you down a flight of stairs while you were at a shopping mall. You have bruises, broken bones, eyewitnesses, and video footage from the security cameras. You and the fifty people that witnessed this all say that they hit you and threw you down the stairs, and the video footage confirms this. There is *still* a solid chance they will deny, minimize, or somehow blame you for this. To see this level of denial can be jaw-dropping.

Their account of events might be something along the lines of, "I didn't do it. That wasn't me." Then the camera footage zooms in and confirms it's them. At that point they might say, "Well, she's making a big deal out of nothing. I never hit her; I hardly touched her. Or, she intentionally landed really hard against that wall in order to get bruises to make me look bad. And I didn't push her down the stairs. We were arguing and I got really close to her and she tripped and fell." Now here is where they finish rewriting reality to make themselves the victim. They'll usually add something like, "She's such a liar and a drama queen. I can't believe I'm going to jail for this; she's ruining my life."

This level of denial or minimization is how and why they feel entitled to abuse and even kill their targets—and it's why they have no remorse about doing so. In their mind they are the victim of *you*. So when a person with such a warped view of events goes into therapy, don't expect them to say, "I got angry, hit my wife, and then threw her down the stairs. I was upset because she picked out a shirt for me that I didn't like. I realize how over-reactive I was, but I didn't see that at the time. Please help me get to the root of my issues so I can treat her with dignity and respect."

An abusive person who is denying or minimizing their behavior isn't going to go into therapy and tell this version--in fact, they are most likely so deluded about their behavior that they are completely unaware that this version even exists.

Even if they are well aware that they are abusive, they may still blame you simply because they enjoy upsetting you. Or, they may seem to fully own their actions and claim that they are sorry and want to change. This is when it's time for you to get clear on where your deal breakers are for this kind of mistreatment. **If a person is physically abusive, please know that the odds of their abuse putting you in the hospital or killing you are higher than the odds of them changing.**

CHAPTER 17

CAN THEY CHANGE?

Promises of Change

I'm including this chapter on change because if you are like most people out there who think they might have a narcissist, sociopath, or psychopath in your life, you are probably wondering if this relationship can be saved. You may have even asked your therapist or looked online for answers, and probably heard that they don't change. For some people this is all they need to hear in order to end their relationship and move on, however, for others, this answer only adds to their confusion.

For those people, the next question that (understandably) follows is, "Well, if they can't change, then how can I be 100 percent certain that they are a narcissist?" The train of logic is they want to make sure that this person in their life is in fact a narcissist before they walk away, and not someone who is "only" difficult, demanding, selfish, entitled, and lacking in empathy and remorse...and who could potential change given enough love, understanding, rehab, or religion.

They might even come across information or professionals that claim that narcissistic or antisocial personality disorder can be cured, which makes them hold onto hope and stay in potentially dangerous situations. This whole train of thought only gets a person off track and stuck in the mud.

The biggest and most helpful question that isn't being asked is *why* the vast majority of mental health professionals don't think that narcissists can change. Because for most of us, the answer of "they don't change, just trust me on this" isn't solid enough for us to end a relationship.

The Stages of Change

So how can we tell if a person (narcissist or not) can, will, or has changed? Well, since we can't look into the future, we can't say for certain. However, what we can do is look at behavior through what's known as "The Transtheoretical Model of Change." This model was developed in the late 1970s by two psychologists, and is currently used by mental clinicians today. This model identifies change as having five stages: pre-contemplation, contemplation, preparation, action, and maintenance. Originally, The Transtheoretical Model was used to describe and understand the process of behavior change with regards to addiction. However, it's a great model that can be applied to any type of behavior that a person wants to start or stop in general. We can use this model to understand where we are in the stages of change, and it allows us to observe someone's behavior and determine where they are in the process of changing as well.

If we shift the questions we are asking, we can get the clarity we are seeking. So, change the question from "Can a narcissist change?" to asking yourself, "Are they ready to change?" "Are they in the process of changing?" or "Have the changed?" Once you understand the stages of change, you'll be able to answer these questions, as well as gain tremendous insight into human behavior.

As we take a deeper look into these stages, remember that we are all going through different stages of change in different areas of our life, and that these stages aren't limited to problematic behavior. I've included examples with each of the following stages so you can better understand this process.

The Five Stages of The Transtheoretical Model of Change

1. Pre-contemplation. In this stage, a person isn't aware, or doesn't acknowledge, that they want or need to change. They haven't given any thought to the possibility of doing anything different, and they do not intend to take any action within the next six months.

No change is possible at this stage. It doesn't matter if we, the police, a judge, or family and friends tell them that they have a problem. If someone doesn't sincerely see an issue with their behavior, then in their mind there is no issue to address, let alone change. If a person denies, minimizes, shifts blame, or justifies their behavior, isn't sincerely and fully accountable, they are in the pre-contemplation stage of change. For those reasons, many people don't ever get to the next stages. If they do, it's fleeting, and they are often apologizing, crying, or taking some sort of massive action in order to keep their relationship going—*not because they are truly remorseful.*

Examples of the pre-contemplation stage:

- A person who doesn't think their alcohol consumption or drug use is a problem.
- A parent who yells, belittles, or hits their children but blames their children for making them act that way.
- A person who is in a dissatisfying relationship, but who hasn't thought about leaving.

*A person in this stage is <u>unaware</u> that a change is wanted or needed.

2. Contemplation. In this stage, a person is thinking about making some sort of change within the next six months. They are weighing the pros and cons about what will be involved if they were to make this change.

In order for any of us to even get to the contemplation stage, we have to experience some sort of physical or emotional pain with staying the same.

For example:

- A person who previously thought their alcohol consumption or drug use wasn't a problem, gets a DUI, gets banned from their local bar, or their partner leaves them because of their drinking. Now they begin to question if maybe their drinking is an issue, and what they can do about it.

- A person in a relationship with someone who yells and belittles them may begin to think about leaving the relationship when that same someone begins to yell and belittle their child.

- A person steps on the scale and is shocked by the number, realizes they need to lose weight and begins thinking how to go about making that happen.

    * A person in this stage is <u>thinking</u> about making a change.

    3. Preparation (Determination). In this stage, a person is ready to take action towards changing within the next thirty days. However, keep in mind that planning to change, isn't the same thing as a person changing. There is an old Chinese proverb that says, "Talk does not cook rice." This proverb says it all.

    When a person is in the planning stage, they are beginning to gather information and resources and working out what kind of steps they need to talk in order to make this change happen.

    A solid plan needs to reasonable, realistic, scheduled, and sustainable. A plan like this includes the elements of who, what, when, where, and how.

    For example, if I say that I want to get sober, or even that I'm going to go to an Alcoholics Anonymous meeting, then this isn't really a plan. This is just talk. This talk becomes a plan when I pick which meeting I'm going to go to, on which day, at which time. So for example, I decide I'm going to take a bus to the AA meeting at the YMCA on the corner of Main Street at 6:30 p.m. this Wednesday. Now that's a viable plan because it includes who, what, when, where, and how. However, for a viable plan to actually last, it needs two more elements: I need to have a motivating reason as to *why* I want to change, and the plan has to be different from anything I may have tried (and been unsuccessful with) before.

The desire to change might be sparked by something outside of ourselves: such as the number on the scale or the threat of losing a relationship. While those shock factors might motivate us to get started, the only thing that keeps us going is if our motivation comes from within. Because if we are only getting sober or into shape because of our partner, and they leave, well, then so does our motivation to get sober.

Additionally, trying to use the same plan that didn't work before without examining why it failed does not count as a viable plan. So, if I've taken the bus to the 6:30 p.m. AA meeting at the YMCA before and I couldn't stick with this plan, then I'll need to examine why and do something different for this to have a chance at working. Because if I try the same plan as before without understanding why that plan failed, then I run the risk of the plan not working again.

If, upon reflection, I realize that what tripped me up before was that I barely had time to get home from work, change, and grab something to eat before I caught the bus, then maybe picking a meeting at a different time might help. Or, if the issue was that I felt really low on weekends, then maybe going to an additional meeting on the weekend might help. If I try making these changes, but am still not successful, then I'll have to keep tweaking my approach until I figure out what works. Maybe that means starting therapy, getting a sponsor, spending time with some friends who don't drink, or maybe it involves a combination of all of the above. You will know what works once you start getting some positive results.

*A person in this stage is <u>planning</u> to make a change.

4. Action. In this stage, a person is actively working towards a change, and is getting their desired results. As with learning any new skill, there is a lot of trial and error as we learn what does and doesn't work for us. Lots of plans tend to fizzle out in the action phase because we either get frustrated with riding the learning curve or we lose motivation for some reason. The biggest challenge with this stage is for us to stay motivated. Reminding ourselves of the pain we will experience if we don't change as well as focusing on the positives our change is bringing can help keep us going.

With a manipulator, you may hear a lot of promises of change. You may even see some action taken. However, this isn't the same thing as a person actually changing. If anything, promises of change and sporadic action result in one of two things:

- They make sudden and radical changes and seem to change overnight...until you let them back into your life when they then revert back to their old selves;

- They are on their best behavior and then you find out, in time, that they've only gotten better at hiding what they've been up to.

* A person in the action stage is *taking action* and is changing.

5. Maintenance. In this stage, we have been taking consistent action, achieving our desired results, and have been able to maintain the change for more than six months. When someone is in this stage, they intend to maintain this change going forward, and work to prevent backsliding.

* A person in this stage has changed and is maintaining their change.

I want to point out two important things about change:

1. Sustained change *only* happens in the maintenance phase. All phases that come before that are just different levels of interest in changing, wanting to change, or taking some action to change. Apologizing, begging for forgiveness, or promising to change are not change. Taking action isn't change. Joining a gym, going to an AA meeting or a therapy session are all great, but they aren't change. Sustained change is the only true change.

2. Change is rarely a smooth process. Change is always difficult, even if we are highly motivated to make it. It can feel like we are continually walking around a mountain with two left feet. *If you were to draw the process of change, you wouldn't see a straight line.* A more accurate picture of change would be a series of circles that go around and around pre-contemplation, contemplation, preparation, action—and sometimes even maintenance, and then it goes back to pre-contemplation. The result is that it would look like a giant scribble. This goes for not just other people, it holds true for all of us. The more savvy manipulators may know this, and may use this to pull on your heartstrings. Please know that's it okay to have your limits with their behavior—in fact, I would encourage you to get clear on where those limits are.

While understanding the stages of change can help us to see the difference between talk, sporadic action, and true change, for those who have a manipulator in their life, trying to tell if they've changed is incredibly difficult. The reason is that they can fake having insight and do a great job at acting the part of having changed. They may cry, beg, plead, apologize, say all of the right things, and seem to show remorse. They may make promises to your children, parents, or people in your inner circle that this time is different. They may get into therapy and start reading self-help books. They may make grand displays of apologizing that would make anyone think that surely they must be sorry because a person who wasn't wouldn't go to such extremes. They may reel you back in telling you that you are their soul mate, and they will do anything to make this relationship work. Don't mistake these grand acts as a sign of sincerity or change. There has to be a point where we say enough is enough—especially if their past behavior shows you that they have no moral compass. Regardless of what they or others might say, you don't owe someone multiple chances to destroy your life.

Changed Behavior Doesn't Fix a Relationship

So often people think that if this other person stopped being manipulative, abusive, drinking or using drugs, that their relationship would be fine. This is not the case. The reality is that there is no relationship present, and there hasn't been one since the damaging behavior came to light—if there ever was a relationship to begin with. Trust, honesty, open, sincere, solutions-oriented communication, respect, and empathy are all necessary ingredients for a relationship. If any one of those elements are missing, there is no real relationship present.

The biggest and most dangerous mistake that targets of manipulation and abuse make is in thinking that the manipulation or abuse is the problem, and if these two things stopped, then everything would be fine. That's not the case. *Maladjusted behavior is there because well-adjusted behavior is missing.* There is no well-adjusted behavior buried inside of the manipulator. Even if they stop their old behavior, they would need to learn new behavior and be willing and able to work to repair the damage done by their previous behavior. In other words, even if they actually changed, this isn't the finish line; this is only the beginning.

Even if the manipulator is sincerely accountable, stops all abuse and addictions, is actively working to restore trust, and is learning more constructive behavior, then the focus would need to shift to the former target. In this step, the former target would need to acknowledge and work through the hurt and anger they have as a result of being on the receiving end of such damaging behavior. This step is ongoing and can take years. It's around this time that the partner realizes that getting the problematic behavior to stop isn't the solution they thought it would be.

PART 3

BREAKING FREE FROM MANIPULATION

CHAPTER 18

SEEING PAIN FOR THE
MESSENGER IT IS

So often we treat both physical and emotional pain as though these uncomfortable sensations are there for no reason. The reality is that pain is our brain's primary way of trying to get our attention so that it can deliver an important message. Just like the navigational system we have on our phone or in our car that lets us know when we need to make a turn or when we are headed in the wrong direction and need to turn around, pain is an important part of our internal navigation system that functions very much the same way. The more we disregard what the GPS is telling us, the further off track we get. Instead of pulling over and taking the time to figure out if we are in fact off track, we've learned to simply turn down the volume and continue driving. This will eventually end up being a problem.

If we didn't experience pain, we would keep doing whatever it is that we are doing. Feeling pain after touching a hot stove is a good thing. If it didn't, we would have no reason to stop touching it. We feel pain because it's our brain's way of getting our attention. Not only is pain an aggressive messenger, it also provides the necessary motivation for us to do something different. If we didn't associate painful consequences to our actions, we wouldn't learn to navigate our environment effectively and would unknowingly continue doing things that cause us harm.

For example, there have been a handful of children born over the years who have a rare genetic disorder known as "Congenital Insensitivity to Pain" (CIP) that prohibits them from feeling physical pain. Parents of these children first start to notice something is different after their child breaks a bone and doesn't seem to notice. No matter how much these parents or doctors stress the importance of being cautious, when pain isn't present, these children are missing the ability to know when to moderate their behavior so they can stay safe. Unfortunately, the life expectancy for a person with this health condition is significantly reduced, and many don't survive into adulthood.

However, many adults without this genetic disorder struggle to fully acknowledge the severity of their pain. When I was working as a nurse, I was continually surprised by the number of people who would come to see the doctor because they were in pain, yet when asked when the pain started, what made it worse or better, and what their pain level was on a scale of zero to ten, ten being excruciating pain, most people didn't know. Or, if they did know, they might have said that their pain was a four; however, the fact that their pain was bad enough to come to the emergency department (their blood pressure or pulse were abnormally high, and they were curled into a ball not wanting to move or talk) said otherwise.

My theory is that in the best-case scenario, this inability to identify pain is due to gender, social, or cultural expectations. By the time we hit puberty, regardless of our gender, most of us learn the lesson that our pain is inconvenient for others, somehow unwarranted, or a sign of weakness. However, these social expectations seem to be especially the case for boys and men, where the message is to "man up" or "stop being a sissy." Additionally, children with parents who were authoritative or abusive also received these messages. When a child in this situation would come in, any question I'd ask them about their pain was either intercepted and answered by their parent or, if the child did answer, they'd make eye contact with their parent in order to get their nonverbal approval before answering. For the record, in situations like this we would try to speak to the child alone and if there was any concern that the child was being abused, it was reported.

I strongly believe toxic gender messages are why boys and men are significantly more hesitant and unable to adequately identify their pain. I would even go so far as to say I think this is why many men who have the early signs of a heart attack, excuse themselves to the bathroom so they can regain their composure, only to never return, whereas women are more inclined to let others around them know that they are in pain or "feel funny."

So if as a society we are so out of touch with distressing physical pain, think about how out of touch we must be with pain that's significantly easier to dismiss, such as emotional pain. Just like with physical pain, we aren't taught to view our emotional pain, or our emotions in general, as the important messengers of information that they are. Instead, we tend to view our emotions as random and unnecessary inconveniences that surface for no valid reason or childish ways of relating to the world that must be replaced with logic and reason. This is a problem.

In order for us to stay out of harm's way we need to be in tune with our emotional pain as much as we need to be with our physical pain. Both types of pain are there to help us navigate life so that we can stay alive. To better illustrate this point, it can help to think of our body as a vehicle and our brain as the computer that runs it. The logical and critical thinking part of our brain functions like a steering wheel, our emotions of pain and pleasure are similar to a GPS and chime at us when we are on or off track, our wants and needs motivate us into action, much like a gas pedal, and when we experience confusion, caution, pain, or fear, these sensations function like a brake pedal. And, of course, what we put into our vehicle matters as well. If we don't nourish ourselves with the right physical, environmental, and mental fuel, our vehicle doesn't get very far. If any one of these key components is missing or if we don't use them in combination with each other, we aren't going to get very far, let alone where we want to go. No wonder so many of us are stalled on the side of the road!

The uncomfortable emotions that accompany emotional pain—such as fear, anxiety, anger, sadness, hatred are there because they have a message for us. If we think these emotions surface for no reason, then we are missing the larger picture and lesson that we need to take a different approach. Because we are all busy and have become so accustomed to being in pain, by the time we reach adulthood, to numb any uncomfortable feelings, we likely aren't even aware that we are in pain and that our lives are severely out-of-balance.

If this imbalance is coming from our inability to know when we need to do more of one thing and less of another, then, in order to feel better, we may start taking a wide range of medications to relieve our anxiety or depression. If we are successful at silencing our pain and the message it's trying to send, our brain will come up with another, usually more intense and not so easily avoided, way to get through to us. I don't intend to over-simplify mental or physical health. Sometimes we really do have a chemical imbalance that can only be corrected with medication. Sorting out what health issues are due to genetics, environment, and suppressed emotions can be quite the challenge.

While not being able to experience physical pain is dangerous, so is not being able to experience emotional pain—for the same reasons. If we don't feel or recognize pain when we should, then we miss out on the message that we need to do something different. It is vital that we feel fear when we perceive danger, anger when we or someone else has been wronged, anxious when we are lacking in stability, sadness when we experience a loss, and empathy when we see another person who is struggling. Without those feelings we would not only struggle to stay safe and keep our lives in balance, but we would struggle to connect to others.

Seeing the Manipulator Clearly

When we are in emotional pain, especially chronic emotional pain, this is a strong sign that something different needs to be done. The emotions of confusion, frustration, and resentment are present when we've had a boundary crossed, and a sign that we need to take some sort of action to protect our boundaries, and thus, ourselves.

If a person's behavior is what's causing us pain, but they don't see a problem with how they treat us, then it's up to us to do something besides trying to cope with being mistreated or hoping they will change. Even if you feel (or actually are) stuck in a relationship with a manipulative or abusive person due to children, illness, lack of finances, or cultural or religious reasons, it's important to change what you can for now in order to bring as much peace and calm as possible into your life—even if this means carving out ten minutes a day to take a hot bath, go for a walk, get to bed a little early, take up a hobby, read before you go to bed, or listen to guided imagery videos.

When We Need to Be the Ones to Change

In order to better see when it's time for us to do something different, I think it's helpful to look at a dynamic we are all familiar with: Lucy and Charlie Brown. While their dynamic is simplistic with nothing major at stake—and a stark contrast to what so many of us have experienced, there is still a lot to be gained from examining what's going on between them.

The cycle these two repeat is that Lucy convinces Charlie Brown to kick a football and offers to hold it for him. Charlie Brown wants to play, but is hesitant, as in the past, Lucy has pulled the ball away causing him to fall and hurt himself. Lucy always reassures him that this time will be different, then she pulls away the ball at the last minute like she always does, laughing hysterically when Charlie Brown gets hurt.

Charlie Brown continues to try and play with Lucy because he keeps hoping this time things will be different and that Lucy will actually hold the ball. Lucy feeds into his hope, and promises that it will. But remember that promising to change isn't change. It's just talk. And the only way for Charlie Brown to tell if this time will be different is to see what happens. For him to continue to take this risk, when the risk is that he'll be hurt, is a dangerous way to determine if she's changed. Charlie Brown can't take Lucy's word that this time will be different, because she's done nothing but lie about that in the past. And worse, she shows no signs of remorse; she finds his pain funny.

The issue here isn't with Charlie Brown's communication. The issue is that unbeknownst to Charlie Brown, they are playing two different games. He wants to play ball, but Lucy wants to play her game of hurt Charlie Brown.

Since she doesn't have a problem with her actions, we can safely say that she's in the pre-contemplation stage. We can tell that she's not going to be changing anytime soon, not only because she doesn't think she has a problem, but also because she laughs every time she pulls the ball away and Charlie Brown gets hurt. She *enjoys* causing him pain. So taking any promises that Lucy makes about holding the ball from this point forward, would be a mistake because she's shown that she isn't trustworthy, and is in fact manipulative and sadistic.

However, because Charlie Brown is still hoping that he'll get to play ball, he doesn't want to see her behavior as the problem it is. The reason is that if he did, then he'd have to stop trying to play the game he so desperately wants to play. Not realizing he's in denial, he views each encounter they have with unwarranted optimism. If anyone were to suggest to him that he needs to do something different, he will most likely be offended, because Lucy is the one with the hurtful behavior, so she should be the one to change. He may also think that if he refuses to give her another chance that he is being judgmental, unforgiving and lacking in compassion—and others around him, who also have poor boundaries, may tell him the same thing.

Charlie Brown is not only in denial but is also misreading the situation by confusing being judgmental with having a healthy degree of discernment, being unforgiving with having healthy deal breakers, and lacking compassion with his ability to be self-protective. His denial is what keeps driving him to give her another chance, and why he continues to feel angry and get physically hurt each time she pulls away the ball. Because he lacks the realization that they aren't playing

198

the same game, coupled with his lack of deal breakers, he continues to try to make an unworkable situation work, wondering what it will take to get through to her. In order for things to change, he's going to have to stop playing this game with her. Until he can let go of the fantasy that playing ball with Lucy will ever be different from what it repeatedly has been and sees reality for what it is, he will be continually disappointed and frustrated by the disconnect between his unrealistic expectations for her behavior and what her behavior really is.

CHAPTER 19

GETTING A GAME PLAN

The idea of developing a game plan may feel overwhelming, as there are quite a few things to consider, however it won't always feel this way. I like to think of it as learning to drive a car that has a manual transmission. At first, there is a lot to learn and to keep in mind at all times. We have to find the balance between the clutch and the gas, know when to up-shift and down-shift, learn how to stop without stalling, avoid popping the clutch, prevent rolling backwards when you are stopped on a hill, and remember to put on the emergency break. With time and practice, we eventually get these skills down.

Believing in yourself, sticking with it, as well as learning to handle feelings of frustration, ineptitude, and discouragement are all part of the process. If you keep at it, a day will come when you realize you aren't nervous and you can drive with ease—you've got these skills down pat, and don't even have to consciously think about what needs to be done. It's second nature. You may not even realize just how far you've come until you see someone else struggling to learn how to drive a stick shift.

Practicing your game plan for how you respond to a manipulator is very much the same way. In time, you will get to the place where responding to them isn't so intimidating or exhausting, and you'll find it hard to remember how and why you interacted with them any differently. Learning and applying any new skill is difficult as first; this is especially so when breaking free from manipulation. However, while change is always painful, so is being used, abused, and exploited. There comes the point where the pain of doing the same thing becomes greater than the pain of changing.

Focus On Understanding the Game and Not Each Tactic

When playing any game, we need to understand what game we are playing, the rules of that game, the moves allowed, and what game pieces are involved. If we are going to win the game, we will need a strategy, and we will need to practice. Manipulators are playing their own game, and they play by their own set of rules that they are continually rewriting to make sure that they win. It's a mistake to try to play baseball if your opponent is playing poker. Manipulators don't play team sports; they are playing an individual sport, and they are playing to win.

Once you start seeing their game for what it is, how you go about playing it will be much easier. However, much like with playing poker, understanding what game you are playing is only half the battle. Realizing that there are different tactics involved, and that they are ever-changing makes all the difference. For this reason, it's vital that we see the whole picture. Focusing solely on individual tactics is a lot like teaching a child to beware of the creepy man in the van who offers candy. Teaching this specific tactic can be helpful ... to a point. After all, what if the stranger doesn't have candy but a puppy? What if the stranger isn't a creepy man, but a friendly woman? What if the stranger isn't a stranger at all, but a family member, a friend, a teacher, or a spiritual leader?

Numerous tactics have been covered in this book, as it's important to be familiar with the wide range of ways manipulator's can come across. However, because every manipulator is different, they won't all come across in the same way. Even the same manipulator will change up their tactics based on what they think will work in that moment. The best example of this is professional poker players. Not only do they play their hand, but they play on the weaknesses of other players. They may pretend to have a weak hand, when they really have a strong one. They may start saying things to intentionally get under the skin of other players in order to get them "on tilt" which means knocked off balance. Good poker players can see this coming, and they prepare themselves the best they can ahead of time. When their opponent tries and fails to provoke them in one way, their opponent will continue to use different approaches until they find one that works, or until they give up. And much like the poker player on the receiving end of this, we too must try to stay as cool, calm, and collected as possible in order to avoid being pushed into becoming reactive.

The Seven-Point Plan to Changing the Game

In order for us to change this game we have been unknowingly playing, we will have to be the one to do things differently. Waiting for the manipulator to change, or attempting to cope with their problematic behavior aren't solid strategies. The seven points that any solid game plan must include are:

1. Understand the game.
2. Understand who your "opponent" is.
3. Understand and Anticipate Your "Opponent's" Moves.
4. Understand who is on your team, (who is safe and who is unsafe) and act accordingly.
5. Understand yourself; understand how you handle stress, what "moves" you tend to make, and why.
6. Develop some strategies.
7. Practice your strategies.

The first three points of this game plan have already been covered in great detail throughout this book. The following chapters go into the remaining four points in greater detail.

CHAPTER 20

UNDERSTANDING AND ANTICIPATING THE MANIPULATOR'S MOVES

Prepare Yourself for the Game

In order to change the game, it's important that you have an idea of what to expect so you can be as prepared as possible. There are seven main points to anticipate so that you aren't so knocked off balance.

1. Expect them to throw out every trick they have in order to pull you back in.

Anytime that a manipulator feels like they are losing control of a situation, they will begin to rapidly shift tactics in order to find one that works. You may see the different masks such as "the charmer" who attempts to re-hook you by telling you everything you want to hear. You may see "the abuser" who verbally or physically pushes you around until you give in. You may see "the intimidator" who threatens that they will never let you leave, get custody, get remarried, sell the house, or work in this town again. You may see the "baby bird with a broken wing" where they seemingly regress in front of your eyes into a wounded child who is so sympathy-inducing you feel bad for holding your ground. You may experience these tactics not just with your partner but, in different variations, with a friend, colleague, business partner, parent, sibling, and so forth.

Seeing all of these masks appear and then morph into the next one can happen within days or even minutes and is one of the most chaotic and confusing things a person can witness. If you have seen this, odds are you were left with the unsettled feeling that you don't really know who this person is.

2. Expect them to play stupid.

They may profess that they didn't know better, or that they didn't mean to hurt you. If you don't see through this, you may find yourself explaining the basics of adult behavior to them. If you find yourself explaining things like what it means to be nice, what flirting is, how lies, deception and betrayal hurt and break trust, or how them yelling, hitting, cussing, or otherwise throwing an adult temper tantrum is not okay, there is a problem. Mature adults do not need these things explained to them, and if they do, they have issues too deep for any basic explanations to solve.

3. Expect them to rapidly push as many of your buttons as possible.

They may go from yelling, to crying, to begging, to showing up at your doorstep, to sending you dozens of emails or text messages, to blocking you on social media, to promising to change, to threatening, to sending you flowers, to name calling, to calling you their soul mate, and to telling you that they never cared about you. It's a wild roller coaster to be on the receiving end of something like this. If they are persistent in telling you everything you want to hear, send you multiple text messages, and call you from different numbers after you blocked them, don't mistake their determination and emotional intensity for sincerity—it's not, it's controlling and obsessive behavior, and has everything to do with them winning, and sucking you back into the cycle of abuse.

4. Expect them to rewrite reality in order to make themselves the victim or the hero.

Manipulators will often try to elicit pity from their target *and those around their target* by talking about their painful childhoods, struggles with addiction, issues with work, family or children, or how hard they've tried in this relationship and how horrible you are to them. They will even try to make you and those around you think you are responsible, or responsible for fixing these problems.

They may also make themselves into the hero. This is done in two main ways: glossing over anything hurtful they've done or flat-out lying about good things they did, that never happened. When a person is being manipulative, they aren't being accountable for their behavior. If they aren't owning what they did, then it makes it a lot easier to deny what they've done. This is how reality gets rewritten. When manipulators gloss over hurtful things they've done, they are now able to focus on how the target wasn't sufficiently grateful for all the ways they were good to them. The result is a dramatically skewed version of reality. For example, you may have filed for divorce because they were controlling, cheating, intimidating, verbally abusive, and/or spending large sums of money without telling you. However, to listen to them tell it, they may say that they never hit you or the children and that they helped take care of you while you were recovering from cancer. While these things might be true, it doesn't mean that their hurtful behavior wasn't the major problem that it is.

When a manipulator flat-out lies about their good deeds, what they say they did *may not even be close* to being true. Much like a child, some manipulators truly live in the reality of their own making. They may tell others that they paid for the children's tuition, went to every soccer match your child played, or helped you pay off your credit card debt. This can be infuriating when the reality is your child had a scholarship, the manipulator never once attended a soccer game, and *you* helped *them* pay off their credit card debt! What's even more wild, is that they can say these things with such emotion and conviction that it seems they actually believe their own lies.

5. Expect them to launch a smear campaign against you.

A smear campaign is a method of damage control that manipulators implement when they are concerned about being caught. However, some manipulators are so deeply dysfunctional, they minimize all of their bad behavior and truly feel that anyone who tries to set boundaries with them is cruel and unreasonable. Regardless, a smear campaign involves them making you look like the problem, and themselves look like the victim.

In terms of romantic relationships, the more intentional manipulators out there often begin a smear campaign on their current partner before their relationship is over. Once this relationship ends, which is usually sudden and for no seemingly good reason, the now former target is left reeling from being discarded in such a cold and calloused way. This pain is devastating enough, but the pain of finding out they've been replaced in lightning-fast speed with a new romantic interest that the manipulator seems so happy with makes an already devastating situation almost unbearable, and it reinforces the target's deepest fears that there was something profoundly wrong with them. This pain grows when they find out that the manipulator is also spreading flat-out lies about them, and people the target thought were friends or were in their corner, now believe, support, or want to stay friends with the manipulator.

A common smear campaign involves portraying the former target as some form of crazy, bipolar, addict, alcoholic, unstable, and/or bad parent. They will then create a series of lies, exaggerations, half-truths, suspicions and false allegations about the target's behavior that serve to undermine the target's credibility. The target often has no idea that a smear campaign has been launched until they begin to experience rude or unusual behavior from others—even friends, family, and their therapists. The people who defend the manipulator and seek to attack the target are referred to as "flying monkeys." Any manipulator, be they a parent, friend, colleague and so forth can orchestrate a smear campaign; the end result for the target can be tremendous amounts of emotional, financial, and social damage.

6. Expect them to send their flying monkeys after you.

The term "flying monkeys" was adopted from the movie *The Wizard of Oz* to describe those that the manipulator sends out to attack the target. In any other circumstance, these flying monkeys may be nice and decent people. However, they've been convinced through either the delusional reality of the manipulator, or the smear campaign that's been launched, that the manipulator is the victim. The manipulator does this by either leaving out everything they've done wrong, greatly minimizing it, or rewriting reality to such an extreme that they claim everything hurtful they did to the target is something the target did to them.

The flying monkeys will respond based on the seeds the manipulator has planted. They may bully, taunt, insult and further break down the target. If the flying monkeys are those who know both the target and the manipulator, such as friends, family, their children, they may become spiteful or pressure the target to give the manipulator another chance. Flying monkeys may initially come into the target's life claiming that they want to be friends or that they care.

They may attempt to enter the target's life pretending to be friendly, but their real intention is to get information out of the target.

If this happens, it's vital that you do not open up to people who haven't proven themselves to be on your side and be emotionally safe. The only way to discern who is emotionally safe and who isn't is by observing their behavior over time. If they are hurtful to you in any way, such as gossiping, teasing you about sensitive issues, sharing what you told them in confidence, or treating you with disdain, contempt, or hostility, then they are not emotionally safe. It's especially important not to open up to anyone who is friends with the manipulator. If you are online and get friend requests from strangers or from those who know the manipulator, you would be wise to decline them. You don't need to figure out what their intentions are. All you need to focus on is that you don't know them, and the odds that they will bring chaos into your life are high. Make it a point from here on out to only keep people with whom you feel safe around in your inner circle.

Additionally, be careful about what you put in writing. A savvy manipulator or their flying monkeys may attempt to provoke you into becoming reactive or giving out information that could be used against you. Assume that whatever you say can and will be used against you either in court or with others. If you are being watched online, or fear that you might be, it is a good idea to create new social media accounts to restore some degree of peace and calm back into your life.

7. Expect that they will "hoover."

There's a term called "hoovering" that's used to describe when a manipulator attempts to reopen contact with the target with the intention of either sucking them back in, or sucking them in long enough so that the manipulator can get a few hateful comments in before they leave again.

Many targets live in some degree of fear that the manipulator they've cut contact with will resurface down the road. I've found that a great way to disable this fear is to lean into it. So expect to hear from them again at some point in the future. This doesn't mean that you have to live in a state of continual hyper-vigilance. What it does mean is now that you have anticipated hearing from them again you can formulate a plan as to how you will respond if this were to happen. I encourage you to keep your emotional shields up if they do contact you. In order to stay strong and hold your boundary, it can help to write out a list of reasons why you cut contact with them in the first place. If you find yourself tempted to contact them or to respond to any contact they make, read your list.

CHAPTER 21

KNOW WHO IS REALLY
ON YOUR TEAM

People who are on your team are supportive of you with both their words and actions. They don't provoke you, stir the pot, seek to agitate, abuse you, or cause chaos. If you have people in your life who are in support of the manipulator, regardless of whether they are family, friends, your children, or your therapist, you would be wise to be careful of what you say around them. There's a solid chance what you say will either be intentionally used against you in some way or unintentionally used to re-victimize you if they begin to justify the actions of the manipulator. One of the most hurtful parts of a manipulative relationship is all of the collateral damage that's done. This will most likely mean either reducing contact with these people, limiting the topics of conversation, or cutting contact with them altogether. It's very rare that a person only needs to get the manipulator out of their life. Usually, radical changes are required across the board.

Many targets come to realize that they will need to cut or greatly reduce contact with those who don't fully support them. If this describes your situation, please know that you aren't over-reacting or being too sensitive. Oftentimes we need distance from all the dysfunction in order to keep ourselves emotionally safe and to heal. When a loved one stays friends with someone who has hurt you, for example, views the manipulation and abuse that was present in your relationship as nothing more than relationship issues, it's normal and appropriate to be upset by this.

If you are someone who is reading this book in an attempt to better understand what a loved one is going through, please know that continuing to stay neutral about what happened, or continuing to be friendly with someone who has mistreated a loved one isn't an act of compassion or maturity; it's invalidating and re-victimizing.

After leaving a manipulative relationship, it helps to start looking at people in your inner circle through a different lens. Before, you may have viewed them in terms of the relationship label—they were your sibling, friend, parent, and so on. However, now, it's important to view them in terms of who isn't emotionally safe to open up to and who is—and to what degree. It doesn't matter if they are your brother, mother, best friend, or spiritual advisor.

Anyone who is on the side of the manipulator, or who is staying neutral by not choosing sides, is not emotionally safe, and the odds that they will share information with the manipulator is very high. I've seen numerous targets over the years be put in harm's way after they've gone to great lengths to escape a manipulator. A primary way this happens is that the target frequently has those in their inner circle who don't understand manipulation or abuse, or how seemingly sincere and persuasive the manipulator can be. What ends up happening is that these often well-intended people let the manipulator know where the target is or how to contact the target because they thought the manipulator had changed. They may think the issue is in the distant past and therefore should no longer be a threat, they feel sorry for the manipulator, or they believe that the target (or their children) should have a relationship with the manipulator, because the manipulator is their parent or some other family member.

If you have moved because you are concerned that you might be in danger, it's important to not give out your address to anyone—at least for the first few years. Instead, it's a good idea to get a PO Box. Some places won't allow you to use a PO Box for your address. For these places, you can use the address of the post office instead. What I do is when someone asks me for my address is that I give them the physical address of the post office along with my PO Box number in this format: 144 W. Ash Street #464. Notice that I don't have the words "PO Box" anywhere in that address. The reason being is I've found that if I give them the address and use the words "PO Box" they are much more inclined to push back and ask for a different address. If I phrase the same address with a street and number, it sounds like an apartment and I don't get the push back. If someone has an issue with that (and sometimes companies do), reiterate that this is the only address you have.

People who are on your team have your best interest in mind at all times, not just when you are around or when they want something. They may be friendly, listen, and act sympathetically, but if they periodically knock you down, say hurtful things to you—or to others about you, then they can't be completely trusted. Those who have never experienced such malicious manipulation or abuse will have a difficult time understanding the lengths you are going to in order to protect yourself. And those who do believe you, but continue to stir the pot by keeping you updated on all of the great things that are happening in the manipulator's life, are being insensitive and hurtful. If you've asserted yourself and told them that you don't want to hear anything about the manipulator, and they continue to disregard your requests, then they aren't respecting your boundaries, and they aren't a friend.

When targets realize they need to start pruning back who is in their inner circle, they often experience a mix of sadness, anxiety, grief, and fear of isolation. This is normal. After all, this is a lot of loss, and it's painful to realize that who you thought was supportive, may not be. I often hear from others that if they got rid of all the problematic people in their lives, there would be no one left. Let me be clear: if the only people you have in your life are problematic, there's no real support there anyway. Believing otherwise is only a false sense of abundance and security. It's like having a refrigerator full of rotten food, trying to convince yourself that you have enough to eat. The good news is that once you get honest about who is and isn't on your team, you can start cultivating new and more supportive friendships.

Well-intended Bad Advice

You may be unintentionally re-victimized by those in your inner circle through well-intended bad advice. This is a problem I've touched on in other parts of the book but will detail here. I go into even more depth on different types of well-intended bad advice in my book, *Out of the Fog*.

What makes this advice so damaging is that it's missing the context of healthy boundaries, and consequently, runs the risk of being dysfunctional, but is passed along as not only truth, but as a healthy way to think and act. If you encounter well-intended bad advice, you may feel confused and upset, but you might not be able to pinpoint why. If you do know why, you may struggle with doubting your boundaries. There is no shortage of well-intended bad advice out there, and it's important that you can see it for what it is so that it doesn't derail you. Listed below are five of the most common and damaging pieces of well-intended bad advice that targets and former targets tend to encounter. This is just an over-view of the main ones; however, there are many more.

Some of the most common pieces of well-intended bad advice that keep people stuck in a fog of dysfunction and manipulation are:

1. Hurt people hurt people.

While there is truth in this, the reality is that this is a simplistic way of understanding hurtful behavior. There are many more factors at play outside of what's happened to a person in their past. After all, we've all been hurt in some way shape, or form. Not all people who have been hurt go on to hurt others. There are far more people out there who have been viciously and violently hurt who don't go on to hurt others. Just because someone is hurt doesn't mean they are somehow justified in mistreating others. Additionally, sometimes people don't hurt others because they've been hurt—sometimes they hurt others because they feel entitled to, society or culture supports and encourages it, or simply because it's fun. Slave owners didn't beat, rape, torture, sell, or kill their slaves because they had a bad childhood. They did this because they saw nothing wrong with it, and worse, neither did tens of thousands of others—including the law.

2. Commitment takes work.

When a person vows to stay married until "death do us part" they are agreeing to this based on the other criteria mentioned earlier in the ceremony, which includes loving and honoring their partner. To say that a person should be expected to uphold this contract even though the other party has broken it, isn't reasonable. Just like with any other contract, if the terms aren't met, the contract is no longer binding.

For example, you are house hunting and find the home of your dreams. The seller tells you that the house is free of mold. You have an inspection done on the home, and it turns out that not only is the house full of mold, but that the seller lied about it and tried to cover it up with paint. You would be well within your right to break this contract and not purchase the house, because the information provided wasn't accurate. Even if you were to buy the house and found out years later that the seller had tried to cover up mold, you could still sue them. It would be ridiculous for someone to expect you to honor this contract, made under false pretenses, by insisting that this is somehow normal and workable because home ownership takes commitment and work.

So yes, while commitment does take work, it takes a certain kind of work: namely, working on spending quality time together, improving communication, building intimacy, and working more effectively as a team. When the saying "commitment takes work" is misapplied in order to push someone to stay in a dysfunctional marriage with a manipulative spouse is not only disrespectful to the person in this manipulationship, it's disrespectful to the institution of marriage.

3. They are doing the best they can; you should be more compassionate.

To be compassionate means to be concerned for the suffering of others. However, it's inappropriate, insensitive, and re-victimizing for a target to be told that they should be concerned about the suffering of their abuser. The focus for the target needs to be on their own healing, which will include them working through many feelings, such as anger over how they were treated, sadness for the relationship they hoped they could have, and remorse for all the time they spent trying to make this relationship work. It's profoundly hurtful and invalidating for anyone to try and push a person into feeling any other way than how they feel.

Additionally, even if the target feels compassion for the person who hurt them, this doesn't mean they need to let that person back into their life. Giving a hurtful person another chance to be hurtful isn't compassionate, it's a sign of poor boundaries. The Dali Lama said it best, "If your compassion doesn't include yourself it's incomplete."

4. You can't heal until you forgive them.

This piece of well-intended bad advice tends to follow closely behind the previous point about targets needing to have compassion for those who hurt them. I am not a fan of the word "forgiveness" as it's so frequently misused and misapplied—often with disastrous consequences. Forgiving another person doesn't mean that we have to be okay with what happened or that we need to let a hurtful person back into our life. The true meaning of forgiveness is to release the anger we are holding at the wrong-doer so it doesn't destroy our lives. However, releasing anger is not an event, it's a process—and for many, the process take years or decades--and some have suffered so greatly that they are hardly able to get through the day let alone work through their anger. And for others, they may fear working through their anger as this is the main thing that is keeping the manipulator out of their life, and, in turn, keeping them safe. Healing from trauma is a process that differs for each of us, and is different for every traumatic experience we encounter. No one else gets to decide what is or isn't traumatic for another person, how they should feel, how they should go about healing, or how long it should take them to heal.

When someone is attempting to make another who is suffering feel better by saying things such as, "In order to heal, you have to forgive them," "Be compassionate, they had a hard childhood," or, "Look on the bright side--things could have been worse," they may think they are saying these things because they care. The reality is these (invalidating) statements are said because they don't like seeing a loved one upset, are akin to telling an upset person to calm down. Caring about a person and not wanting to see them upset are two different things. However, because, as a society, we aren't taught how to handle uncomfortable emotions—ours or anyone else's, we often don't know how to show someone we care other than to try to get them to feel better. When someone tries to get us to feel differently than we currently do, this doesn't make us feel better—it makes us feel invalidated, enraged, or embarrassed for feeling the way we do. This isn't what a person who is suffering needs. What is helpful is to give them the room to feel how they feel and to work through those feelings as they surface.

Being consumed by grief can feel very much like being out in the middle of the ocean at night. Each emotion surfaces like a giant, unseen wave, catching us off guard, hammering and pushing us under with its intensity, leaving us fearful that we won't be able to resurface, and if we do, that we can't withstand the next one. With time and support, the sun does rise, the ocean becomes less overwhelming, and these waves lessen in strength and frequency. For those who have healed from a trauma of any kind, they never "got over" how they felt they had to *go through* each of their feelings as they surfaced. This means that they have made some degree of peace that these waves are a normal part of the ocean that is grief, and they are now better able to see these waves coming, and can surf them to shore.

CHAPTER 22

UNDERSTANDING HOW YOU HANDLE CONFLICT AND STRESS

In order to develop some effective strategies for interacting with difficult people, it can be helpful to better understand how the human brain reacts under stress.

We often think that we have one brain, but the reality is that we have three brains that have evolved over time. These three brains are known as the "reptile brain," the "mammalian (or dog) brain," and the neocortex or "new brain." The "reptilian brain" is the oldest, and involves all activities that keep us alive such as our fight, flight, freeze defenses, as well as helping to regulate our temperature, appetite, breathing, and sexual desires. The "mammalian brain" is the largest part of our brain, and is the seat of our emotions. Some of its functions include making value judgments, and remembering pleasant and unpleasant experiences. The neocortex is the newest part of our brain and is what sets us apart from other mammals. It controls language, speech, abstract thought, and our ability to think ahead and plan for the future.

When our fight, flight, or freeze defenses are activated, our neocortex, or the thinking part of our brain, is greatly diminished or goes offline completely, and our behavior is now being driven by our reptilian and mammalian parts of our brain. This results in us being impulsive, reactive, or unable to move or speak. We don't have to experience a major threat to feel this way. Giving a speech, going on a first date, or facing a person we find intimidating can all trigger these defenses. When we are in fight or flight mode, we aren't thinking clearly, if at all.

Once you understand how you tend to handle stress and pressure, your life will radically start to change, especially once you are able to develop more empowering ways to respond. Everyone handles conflict, confrontation, fear, and stress differently. However, when a threat is perceived, our responses tend to go into fight, flight, freeze, or "friend" mode, with the first response usually being freeze. Understanding what it feels like and how you normally behave when you go into fight, flight, or freeze can allow for a lot of insight. I also hope that it can allow for self-compassion when you don't handle stressful things the way you wanted.

Fight, Flight, Freeze, and Friend

Freeze Mode

In terms of being around manipulators, we tend to go into freeze mode when they say or do something that knocks us off balance. For example, they might make an inappropriate request, do a 180 and switch from being nice to being mean, or, switch from being mean to being kind or considerate. When this happens, our brains are trying to process a lot of conflicting information. And much like a computer that is trying to process more data than it is equipped to handle, all of our brain's energy is being directed to sort out what's going on and why. The result is that we are left feeling stunned, at a loss for words, and potentially unable to move. If we are able to say or do something, fear may take over, and we find ourselves becoming eager to please by agreeing to requests or demands that we wouldn't have otherwise done had we not been knocked off balance. People-pleasers are notorious for defaulting into saying yes because they aren't comfortable with conflict or confrontation of any kind.

Flight Mode

When we go into flight mode, we are not reasonable or rational. When panic sets in, we are in a scramble and seek to get away by all means necessary. Think of how a deer reacts when they get startled. They take off running and don't stop until the fear subsides. When they are running, they are less concerned about what's in front of them or where they are going, and more concerned about getting away from whatever they found threatening, which is why they may run into traffic. People behave in a similar way. Instead of running through the forest, we may flee in a wide number of ways. When panic sets in, we might leave the room, change the topic, avoid the person or situation, or we might seek to escape into watching TV, shopping, drugs, alcohol, computer games, work, you name it.

Fight Mode

When fight mode takes hold, our brain "downshifts" and our basic instincts take over, and the critical thinking, empathy and remorse parts of the brain go offline. It's also worth noticing when other people (especially the manipulator in your life) are in fight, flight, or freeze mode so that you can adjust your behavior accordingly. For example, you do not want to try and reason with someone who is in fight mode. Their thinking brain is offline, and they are running off of adrenaline and their emotions. Additionally, when someone is in fight mode, the parts of the brain that control empathy, the desire to connect and bond to others, or to reach a solution are not present—especially if they are exhibiting aggression towards you. So it's important for you to not to expect someone who is aggressive to be logical, reasonable, or caring during times like these. I'm not saying that you should get better at tolerating this kind of behavior, I am saying to see their behavior clearly so you can take the self-protective actions necessary.

"Friend" Mode

Friend mode isn't a standard defense like fight, flight, or freeze, but it's what many people-pleasers do as an attempt to get through stressful situations. When a person goes into friend mode, their voice tends to become higher, they become overly complimentary and are quick to take a submissive role, giving into the demands of the person they find intimidating. Author Pete Walker was the first person I came across to identify this "friend" mode, although he refers to it as "fawn" (as in fawning over someone). I find his insight about this defense to be spot-on and highly relevant to all of the people-pleasers of the world who may default into a freeze-and-friend mode instead of fight-or-flight.

Examining Your Default Behavior

So now that you know the different default ways that stress is handled, it's time to examine what triggers each of these defenses in you. While these defenses are a reactive response that often catches us off guard, with enough self-awareness and practice you can change your behavior to where you become more responsive. This doesn't mean you won't still feel panic; it means that you'll be better able to channel that fear into constructive action.

It's worth reflecting on different responses you've had in the past so that you can become familiar with your default responses and can build a plan around them. For example, if you tend to go into freeze mode and can't think of anything to say, then a good plan would be one where you incorporate this knowledge. This might mean that your plan needs to include getting some distance and space so you can shift out of freeze mode and so your thinking brain can come back online. A good way to do this is to go to the bathroom and run cold water over your hands, which can help bring you back to the present moment. You can always go back and address whatever issue they or you have once you are feeling more centered. And you might want to do this through email so you have a paper trail as well as so they don't continually knock you off guard.

The other option is to practice and prepare a different response ahead of time. This strategy can be effective, but I highly recommend you practice working around what you know about your default defenses first. If and when you decide to practice different responses, it can help to rehearse them with a trusted friend or therapist. Make sure to include in your role playing things the manipulator might say to throw you off balance, and come up with responses as well as remaining as cool, calm, and collected as you can. Practicing under pressure is how and why firefighters, emergency medical teams, and other types of first responders train the way they do. This is because regardless of how well we know our skills, how we think we would act during a crisis and how we actually act are often two very different things. It's important to get the skills down, but it's also important to train for getting the right responses down so we can try to prevent defaulting into either inaction or reaction.

CHAPTER 23

UNDERSTANDING YOUR VULNERABILITIES

At the core of every action we take, there is some sort of need we are trying to meet. However, *oftentimes these needs are below our conscious level of awareness.* The more we can bring our hidden motivations to the surface, the better chance we have at breaking problematic patterns.

Psychologist Abraham Maslow categorized a variety of human needs into a hierarchy with five levels. This hierarchy is normally shown as a pyramid, but functions more like a ladder, with level one being at the bottom and level five being at the top. Here are those five different levels in more detail:

Level 1: Physiological needs of food, clothing, sleep, and shelter.

Level 2: Safety needs, which include security, stability, a sense of control, order, and freedom from fear.

Level 3: Love and belonging needs, which include friendship, intimacy, trust, and a sense of connection.

Level 4: Esteem needs, such as achievement, independence, and the desire to get respect from others.

Level 5: Self-actualization needs, which include personal growth and the desire to reach our fullest potential.

We can't advance up the ladder of this hierarchy until our more basic needs are met. For example, if someone is going through a divorce, their needs of shelter, stability, sense of connection, love, and belonging will most likely all be uncertain. These needs are all found on levels one, two, and three. Consequently, their attention will be on getting those needs met before they would be able to focus on their level four and five needs of building their self-esteem or enhancing their personal development.

I find it helpful to view Maslow's hierarchy in the more general sense of "buckets" that need to be filled. So, we have the buckets for our physical needs (food, clothing, shelter), emotional needs (affection, attention, importance), safety and stability needs (the reassurance that our physical and emotional needs will continue to be met on a consistent and predictable basis); esteem needs (self-confidence, self-direction, self-worth) and self-actualization needs (striving to become our highest and greatest self).

When one (or more) of our needs is not met, that bucket gets low. When that happens, we are in a scramble trying to get it filled, although we most likely won't realize that we are in a scramble. After a major life change such as a divorce or death, we may get the advice to make no major decisions. The reason is because we aren't thinking clearly, *but we don't realize it.* Any decisions we make at this time will often be an impulsive attempt to get these basic needs met, which often results in poor decision making.

The degree to which a person's buckets are empty tends to be in direct proportion to the degree of a scramble they are in... and the emptier the bucket the worse their judgment will be. When we are in a scramble, our thinking switches from being rational to *rationalizing,* which is a problem.

Our buckets are being continually filled and emptied as we move through life. A person can start off life with parents who, due to any number of reasons, were not able to meet their needs (fill their buckets) effectively. Maybe their parent struggled with addiction or untreated mental illness, maybe they were a workaholic, or for whatever reason, were unable to be emotionally or physically available for their child to the degree that the child needed. *If a child starts out life with a low or empty bucket, they are going to take that into adulthood.* When you hear talk of childhood wounds, these wounds stem from buckets not being filled—or, in the case of a traumatic event, these buckets were emptied. However, because our buckets need continual filling and monitoring, they can also get emptied later on in life. So a person may have had a wonderful childhood, and then some traumatic event, (such as the death of their spouse, bankruptcy, foreclosure, divorce, loss of a job or even turning a certain age) can cause their buckets to get low and result in driving their behavior.

Here are some examples of some common empty buckets and the kinds of rationalizing thinking that go along with them:

Emotional-needs bucket: A person grows up feeling unloved or unimportant making them vulnerable to what's known as "love bombing" and the whirlwind romances, friendships, and business partnerships/dealings that emotional manipulators create. They will most likely find themselves in a series of one-sided friendships and relationships with emotional manipulators who take them for granted, abuse and/or exploit them. The target may be willing to stay in this dynamic because, when the emotional manipulator is so attentive and affectionate (not to mention charming!), the target's emotional-needs bucket is overflowing.

Safety-and-Stability-needs bucket: A person frequently relocates as a child and now craves stability as an adult, even if the price of that stability means staying in an unhealthy relationship, friendship, or even job. This generally means the situation must become intolerable or dangerous before they are willing to leave. When we feel fear, we cling to what we know in order to stay safe in the moment—even if what we feel is safe is actually dangerous in the long-term. The result is that we feel this is the one and only job/friendship/relationship where we can meet this need, and we become panicked by the idea of losing what we have.

If we don't work toward identifying and filling our empty buckets in a healthy way, we will struggle to identify and set boundaries with problematic people and situations. We may then feel powerless over preventing being hurt and begin to isolate ourselves in an attempt to stay safe.

Examining Your Vulnerabilities

When our buckets stay low or empty for a long period of time, they become vulnerabilities that drive our behavior and negatively influence our decision making—without us even realizing it. When we can't discern the difference between the emotionally or physically safe and unsafe behavior of others, we gloss over red flags and assume good intentions when there aren't any. This results in us unknowingly chumming the waters for predatory people by giving them multiple chances to hurt us, whereas a person who is able to discern these differences distances themselves immediately. I don't say this to scare you; I say this to prepare you.

Remember, manipulation is only effective if we don't see it for what it is and we don't know how to respond to it once it starts. We will always have vulnerabilities, and they will grow and change as we grow and change, so it's important for us to continually assess them. Having vulnerabilities isn't a bad thing; it's part of being human and what helps us to empathize with others. *Our vulnerabilities become a problem when we aren't aware of them, when they drive our behavior, and if we can't tell when they are being exploited.*

For example, after my own experiences with emotional and psychological abuse, I started an online support group to help others. Initially, I expected a few dozen people at the most. Our group blew past that number on the first day. Five years later, we now have over fifty-thousand members, and the group averages over 150,000 responses a month. I mention this because I'd have to really have my head in the sand to not see patterns of behavior arise. One of the biggest patterns I've seen is that members frequently get caught up with numerous problematic people who manipulate, cheat, steal, or abuse before they are able to break free once and for all.

The main factor is that they continue to misread and gloss over the behavior of others and struggle to hold the standard of being treated with dignity and respect. Maybe they were abused or neglected as children, and consequently, being treated with a lack of dignity or respect and continually glossing over problematic behavior, is normal and doesn't register as the huge issue that it is. Maybe they were in an abusive relationship before, but because they are fearful of being alone or missing out on a great partner, they chalk up any concerns they have with other people's behavior as them being hyper-vigilant as a result of their last relationship, and they are quick to dismiss any concerns they have.

My favorite part of running that group is seeing people make the shift back into trusting themselves and cultivating a healthy level of discernment when it comes to others. The next chapter on boundaries, standards, and deal breakers goes into this in much greater depth.

So while understanding manipulators and common manipulations can be helpful, *the most beneficial thing you can do is to examine what your unmet needs are. If these unmet needs were exploited in the past, then it's vital to examine what hooks enticed you.*

The reason is that if these soft spots are still unknown to you, there's a solid chance they are unconsciously driving your behavior, and you run the risk of being exploited in a similar way in the future. I say this because I see a lot of people on the road to healing become hyper-focused on trying to understand narcissists or sociopaths thinking that if they can understand everything about them, that will keep them safe. Understanding problematic people and behavior will only keep you safe to a point. Understanding *yourself* is where your power is and what will truly set you free.

CHAPTER 24

EXAMINING YOUR SELF-ESTEEM AND FREQUENTLY EXPLOITED PERSONALITY TRAITS

The term "low self-esteem" brings up many different thoughts and ideas. Some people might think that if a person has low self-esteem this means they don't like what they see in the mirror, or that they are insecure and don't feel good about themselves. And that would be accurate for some; however, low self-esteem runs much deeper than what we consciously think about ourselves--it's how we treat ourselves and where we set our standards for how we feel we deserve to be treated.

I've come across countless targets who think they have healthy self-esteem. They have an accurate view of themselves as well as their strengths and weaknesses and overall feel good about who they are. However, because they don't walk around hating themselves, they don't see how their self-esteem could play a part in why they are continuing to date or befriend manipulative or abusive people. The truth is that a big part of healthy self-esteem is treating our time, energy, money, body, and space with value, knowing when and how to set boundaries for what is harmful to us, and not staying in a potentially dangerous situation waiting for them to hurt us (or to have concrete proof that they are hurting us) before we leave.

Additionally, even if a target had healthy self-esteem before getting involved with a manipulator, the odds are that their self-esteem has been damaged in ways they aren't yet aware of. However, by the end of this chapter, you will have a solid start on identifying some key areas that may need some attention.

The Two Basic Types of Self-Esteem

There are two types of self-esteem out there: type 1 and type 2.

A person with a type 1 self-esteem expects to be treated with dignity and respect, and believes there is no justification for others to treat them poorly. If another person lashes out at them or treats them poorly in any way, they don't accept justifications for being mistreated. It doesn't matter if the other person had a bad day, a bad childhood, or was frustrated or angry with them. If someone mistreats them, they assert themselves and make their boundaries known. They also expect the other person to be accountable for mistreating them. If this other person continues to mistreat them, then they distance themselves. They value themselves and don't spend time trying to justify their value to abusers or anyone else who doesn't see it.

A person with a type 2 self-esteem justifies being mistreated by others. They often feel taken for granted and unlovable. When others mistreat them, they believe they are to blame, and work hard to change their behavior so that the relationship will work. However, all this hard work seems to only yield crumbs of niceness, honesty, or loyalty from others—if that. Deep down they don't feel lovable, and because of this they cling to any relationship no matter how unfulfilling or abusive because they think this is as good as things can get for them. They confuse their niceness with being boundary-less, and don't understand why they are continually taken for granted when they are so loving, forgiving, and considerate. They frequently have crazy-makers and abusers in their life—which only reinforces their low self-esteem and feelings of worthlessness and helplessness.

Knowing which type of self-esteem you currently have and have been operating from can be very eye-opening, and can go a long way toward setting you free.

Three Results of Low Self-Esteem

1. Continual self-doubt. If you distrust your judgment and perceptions of people and situations, then odds are you look to others to take the lead on what you should think, feel, or how you should act. This is how people tend to get involved in a series of abusive relationships. They doubt themselves, think any misgivings they have about someone are due to their PTSD or previous relationships with abusers, and then they either ask the abuser or those around them for reassurance. Not being able to trust your perception of others or of events is a problem, especially if the new person is manipulative or abusive.

If you are continually unsure and need the validation or direction from others, then odds are one of two things will happen: you will either be continually anxious and fearful when it comes to making a decision, or you will have perpetual regret as to why you listened to what someone else thought you should do. *You must know yourself to be yourself.* Becoming your own counsel and following your own course is vital, as deep down, you know what's best for you. You really do. It's okay to ask for input from others, but it's vital that you are able to ultimately form your own opinion. Learning to validate yourself takes time, but it can be done. It helps to start by making small decisions, remind yourself that you control the pace and can get distance when you need to. Additionally, it helps to think about someone that you've known for a while and with whom you do feel safe around (perhaps a trusted sibling or family member, friend, or therapist). Think about how you feel around them, and use this feeling as a reminder that you don't always feel anxious around people.

2. Low degree of self-protection. If you are continually placing your safety and sanity last, or can't tell when you are being mistreated or in danger, then this is not only a problem—it's incredibly dangerous. This is especially the case if the other people you are making a priority are manipulative or abusive. All animals have protective instincts and would easily be picked off by predators if they didn't. Humans are no different.

Here are some signs that your ability to be self-protective needs work:

- You can't tell the difference between a safe person and a dangerous person.

- You are quick to drop any and all boundaries if someone is nice, attractive, friendly, or funny.

- You trust others completely upon meeting them and think that doing anything less than this means you have trust issues or are hyper-vigilant.

- You look to others to validate your decisions before you take action—no matter how problematic they are, or how major the situation is.

- When you have concerns about someone's behavior, you automatically assume that your instincts are wrong. You then interact with them as though they don't have concerning behavior, giving them the benefit of the doubt until their behavior proves that they are in fact untrustworthy or dangerous.

- You keep abusive or destructive people in your life thinking that they would never hurt you like they have others—that your relationship with them is special and different.

- You continually go back to a person who has threatened or harmed you thinking that your love can fix them.

You matter just as much as anyone else. Putting yourself in harm's way to try and save someone who doesn't want to be saved—or worse, who wants to hurt you so that they can feel better about themselves or get their way—is a huge problem that can cost you your life.

3. External locus of control. A locus of control is how and where you attribute the cause of things that happen or don't happen to you. There are two types of locus of control: internal and external.

If a person has an external locus of control, they feel that their life is largely directed by things outside of their control—usually other people. This external focus causes a person to become angry, bitter, jaded, defeated, helpless, depressed, anxious, distrusting, and fearful.

A person with an internal locus of control is largely self-directed. They understand what they have control over and what they don't. They feel capable of implementing positive change in their life, and as a result feel empowered. Shifting to developing an internal locus of control starts with getting in tune with your emotions and discerning what is safe and unsafe as well as nourishing and draining for you. Once you have a better grasp on these things, it will be easier to develop boundaries, standards, and deal breakers around them.

Ask yourself: *Do you have any of the above personality traits? If so, take a moment to list them and give some examples as to how this has been a problem in your life. Where do you think they came from?*

Frequently Exploited Personality Traits

While anyone can be the target of a manipulator, those who tend to get caught up with multiple manipulators generally do so because they have certain personality traits that are impacting their ability to be self-protective—which makes them vulnerable to exploitation.

These four traits are: going with the flow (people pleasing), fear of anger, desire to avoid conflict or confrontation, and no solid sense of self. The challenge for those with these certain traits is that because they've always been this way, and because these traits are mistaken by ourselves and others as ideal behavior, it can be difficult to see the problem when it's masking itself as the solution. Additionally, some of these traits may be the foundation for their personality and what's made them successful in certain areas. When low self-esteem is present, a person has these four different traits to an extreme.

Some of these traits you may not have even been aware of, while others such as going with the flow and avoidance of conflict or confrontation may have served you well your whole life...until now. After all, in a healthy context, many of these actions, especially getting along with others, are seen as desirable. However, like anything else, considerate and kind behavior can become problematic if taken to an extreme (this usually happens if a person is putting everyone else first and themselves last). Most of us don't ever take the time to examine our seemingly good behavior, because we don't see it as a problem. And most of us tend to think we have healthy thinking and boundaries ... until we get a manipulator in our lives who creates so much chaos and confusion that we are confused as to how things got this bad and how we didn't realize what was happening.

Here are the four personality traits that are frequently exploited:

1. Going with the flow. Being easy-going and working well with others is great to a point. If this personality trait is taken to the extreme of continually pleasing others, then this leads to an imbalance in all of our relationships. Ingratiating ourselves and avoiding confrontation does not make for a healthy relationship, it makes for resentment and a buildup of issues.

If we feel a compulsive need to please others, we may feel out of control and frustrated with our life, because our actions are limited to what is considered acceptable by others. Perpetually pleasing others causes harm—especially if we are taking care of everyone else at the expense of ourselves. Many people pleasers use "niceness" as a way to subconsciously protect themselves from being abandoned. Others go with the flow because being nice is a core part of their identity. This is also problematic, as the need to be seen (or see yourself) as nice can keep you from being assertive. We may find ourselves too "nice" (passive) to confront or criticize a manipulator, or too "nice" (in denial) to see their problematic behavior for what it is.

Some examples of people pleasing:

- Going along with others to get along with them.
- Saying "yes" when you mean "no."
- Setting a boundary makes you feel guilty or selfish.
- Having no opinion or not knowing how you feel about a person or situation.
- Trying to prove your worth.
- Being willing to change things about yourself (grinding yourself down, turning yourself into an emotional pretzel, physically changing to make others happy) so that others stay in your life or approve of you.

Not everyone will like you, and even if they do, they won't approve of everything you are doing all the time. This is one of the many reasons it's important to know yourself well enough that you can stand firm in your decisions. If you always need others to be okay with your actions, you are going to be waiting a very long time. You need to approve of your own behavior. It can help to realize that of all the people out there, ten percent will never like you, ten percent will love you, and eighty percent will fall somewhere in between.

Trying to please others thinking that other people will treat you like you treat them isn't a good strategy. Using niceness as a way to avoid being abandoned or to keep you safe from harmful people, tends to do the exact opposite: *it will make you a continual target for hurtful and harmful people.*

There is nothing wrong with needing some reassurance from time-to-time, but it becomes a problem when their approval becomes essential to your self-esteem, and the lack of approval causes you to become anxious, unhinged, and in a panic. If you are trying to avoid being left, then you will go to great lengths to keep others around, regardless of how poorly they treat you. However, if you are trying to keep the peace with others so they don't leave but doing so is at the expense of never disagreeing with them or being able to share what you really think and feel, then you will end up starting a war within yourself.

While it's essential to learn how to say "no," it's also important to be aware of what you are saying "yes" to, and the tone that it is setting. For example, you may have no issue with getting your coworkers a cup of coffee, running errands for your boss, continually letting others decide which restaurant to go to, or meeting someone at their house for a first date, but be aware that what you say "yes" to sets a tone for how others will perceive and treat you. It may not be right or fair, but it's reality.

2. Fear of anger. Most team-oriented people want peace in their lives. However, there is a difference between resolution of conflict and avoidance of conflict. If a person is attempting to avoid conflict, they may try to avoid anger, aggression, conflict, and confrontation within themselves and with others. These suppressed emotions don't go away; they will resurface in ways that we are comfortable in acknowledging. For example, we may suppress our anger at our spouse, but then that anger surfaces in the form of physical symptoms such as chronic pain, headaches, or weight gain. Or perhaps it comes out in passive-aggressive ways such as burning their dinner, forgetting to pay bills, or being messy.

People pleasers are often uncomfortable with anger—either theirs or someone else's. They may not know how to be angry in an appropriate way, and so they may feel it's safer to bottle up that anger and pretend that everything is fine. We all get frustrated and angry. It's how we handle those emotions that makes all the difference. It's okay for a person to feel how they feel; however, it's not okay for a person to become cruel or hurtful.

3. No solid sense of self. People who have no solid sense of self define themselves through the opinions and approval of others. A person without a solid sense of self is quick to give away their power to others as they think that everyone else knows better than they do—even regarding their major life decisions.

If we don't have a solid sense of who we are, then we also don't know our thoughts, feelings, emotions, and core values, and are ripe for manipulation. Alternatively, if we do know who we are, but our identity is limited to only being a healer or caregiver to others, then this is also a problem, as we will continue to not only find the proverbial baby birds with broken wings, but we will unconsciously seek them out. Many empaths, codependents, and "born healers" are often very in tune with others, and very out of tune with themselves. Their thoughts and feelings are often blurred with others', so much so that they can't tell whose is whose. Having empathy for others doesn't mean that we need to have a lack of boundaries.

One of the first steps in developing a solid sense of self is to get reconnected with who you *really* are. Here are some questions that can start you down the path of better understanding yourself:

- What are some of your strengths?
- What are some of your weaknesses?
- In what ways are you a friend to yourself?
- In what ways are you an enemy to yourself?
- When was the last time you had your feelings hurt? What happened?
- How are you feeling right now, and why?
- What decision (if any) have you been hesitant to make and why?
- How can you tell (physically and emotionally) when you are stressed out? What do you do to manage stress?

- What are two things you've learned about yourself lately?

4. Desire to avoid conflict or confrontation. If two people are being open with their thoughts, feelings, and opinions they will experience conflict from time-to-time. How that conflict is handled is what determines if this is a solutions-and team-oriented dynamic or not. If you are the one who continually gives in or does all the work to get things back on track, then there is an unequal balance of power, and most likely a one-sided dynamic in more ways than you may realize. If both people involved have open, honest, sincere, and solutions-oriented communication, then handling conflict doesn't have to end in a shouting match or the relationship ending; assertive communication can be used to resolve the conflict. *Avoiding conflict or not having any conflicts isn't a sign of a healthy relationship; it's a sign of poor communication.*

CHAPTER 25

BOUNDARIES, STANDARDS,
AND DEAL BREAKERS

Boundaries, standards, and deal breakers are vital to living an authentic life. In combination, they allow us to determine what we let into our life and what we keep out. If we lack any or all of these, we are in harm's way and don't even realize it.

Before we dive into the importance of boundaries, it's crucial to understand that attempting to set boundaries with an abusive person can lead to their behavior escalating and becoming very dangerous very fast. Remember, everything is a power struggle with them, and they play to win. Trying to have open, honest, sincere, solutions-oriented communication with a manipulative person doesn't work—and it often makes things worse. Always make your safety a top priority; err on the side of caution, and don't take any advice from me or others that you feel would put you in harm's way. You know your situation the best.

If you are involved with a dangerous person who harms you physically, emotionally, mentally, spiritually, sexually, socially, or financially—*the only boundaries that will keep you safe are physical and emotional distance.* Continually trying to explain to them what they've done wrong, why it's wrong, and why it hurt you is as effective as screaming into the wind, and it can put you in serious danger. Remember, you are dealing with a person who is intent on winning, not a person who works as a team. Anyone who purposefully harms you in any way *will not* respect you or your boundaries. If anything, they will see your boundaries as a challenge for them to conquer.

Boundaries

Boundaries are more expansive than saying yes when we mean yes, and no when we mean no--although that's a good start. The best definition I've ever heard of boundaries comes from codependency expert Pia Mellody in her book, *The Intimacy Factor.* She describes boundaries as, "a form of both *containment and regulation* to where we are able to express ourselves moderately *as well as* are able to filter incoming messages from others in a self-protective way." In other words, our boundaries are a semi-permeable layer, much like a cell wall that only allows for what is appropriate to enter and exit. When our boundaries are functioning properly, we don't get hurt and we don't hurt others. While healthy boundaries won't protect us from all harm, they do protect us the vast majority of the time.

For example:

A person with a functional *external* containment boundary is one who can contain and control their behavior. When they get upset, they are able to restrain themselves from lashing out at others.

A person with a functional *internal* regulation boundary is able to regulate what types of communication and actions they let in from others. If someone were to yell at them or call them names they would see this abusive anger as a reflective of the other person's issues--not as the truth about them. After all, "normal," well-adjusted people don't go around trying to destroy others. If they have their feelings hurt, they make sure to keep those hurt feelings and their self-worth in two different buckets.

A great way to tell if your boundaries, standards, and deal breakers need some work is to honestly evaluate your feelings and actions. Have you been feeling resentful or angry towards a particular person? Have you been gossiping, complaining, or "venting" to others about this person? If you answered yes to either one of these questions, then odds are you've had a boundary crossed or completely violated. When we stew or vent, it's because the issue hasn't been effectively resolved. If the person we are upset with is someone who is willing and able to work towards resolving issues with us, then an assertive, tactful conversation will most likely be able to get things back on track. If an honest conversation cannot correct this imbalance, or only makes it worse, then it's time to go into self-protection mode and limit what we share, or how much time we spend around them.

Many people are uncomfortable with setting healthy boundaries because they don't want to be rude, or they fear confrontation, rejection, disapproval, or abandonment. They may believe that if they set boundaries with others, this will cause them to miss out on a potentially wonderful person or that they will be alone forever. These fears often have their roots in childhood, and are the result of getting the message that in order to be loved, we have to behave in a way that they see fit—because who we are isn't good enough, and to be ourselves means to be rejected.

The result of not having boundaries is that our relationship dynamics with significant others, family, friends, and co-workers all become one-sided. We silence who we are and lose ourselves to the wants, needs, and opinions of others, looking to them to tell us who we are and how we should think and act. Anyone who disrespects your boundaries will become increasingly problematic for you if they remain a significant part of your life. And if we are turning to a pathological person for validation, then we will see a deeply flawed version of ourselves reflected back at us through their eyes, and we will mistake it for the truth. The consequence of these one-sided, unfulfilling relationships where we are more focused on pleasing other people than valuing ourselves is a life full of anger, hurt, and resentment, although it may take many years for us to even realize we feel this way.

Setting boundaries is necessary for emotional intimacy to develop with others. And yes, setting boundaries will turn off some people. That's okay. Not everyone you meet is meant to be in your life, let alone in your inner circle. Removing people from your life, or moving them to a different circle in your life, is often difficult at first, but it's a lot easier than living a life of misery and invalidation with an inner circle full of all the wrong people. This process is significantly easier if we can work towards meeting new people or cultivating nourishing friendships while we are pruning off the old ones.

Since everyone's boundaries are different, and are in an ever-evolving state, no one knows where another person's boundaries are unless they make them known. For example, we all have different senses of humor in different environments. What one person finds funny, another finds distasteful. If we don't find a certain type of joke funny, it's doesn't mean it's because we are too sensitive. It means we don't find certain topics humorous, or we are only okay with certain jokes from certain people. After all, how we joke with a friend is different than how we joke with a stranger on the subway or a coworker we hardly know.

Let's say someone tells a joke we find inappropriate, and we don't laugh or we tell them we don't find jokes like that funny. If the other person didn't mean to offend us, they will most likely apologize and not tell us jokes like this in the future. If they don't care that they offended us, they don't have respect for our boundary, and will most likely try to convince us that their joke is funny, tell us we are too sensitive if we disagree, and then continue to tell us more jokes like this in the future.

If we don't have a solid footing in our boundary, we are going to think they are right about us being too sensitive and not having a good sense of humor—and our self-esteem will take a hit. If we are grounded in our boundary, we will hold our ground and tell them we don't like jokes like this. We won't internalize their comments about us being too serious or uptight, because we are comfortable in our boundary. If anything, the more they continue to fight us about our boundary, the more clarity we have that their behavior is disrespectful and immature—and doesn't have anything to do with us. They can think whatever they want to think, but because we are okay with our boundary, we don't take their comments to heart and as a result, our self-esteem stays intact.

While others may not know where our boundaries are, it is reasonable to expect another adult to behave in a situationally appropriate and respectful way towards you and others. If someone is being too touchy-feely, rude, deceptive, or abusive, you don't need to stand there and assert yourself until they finally learn they need to treat you with respect. Putting yourself in harm's way like this in order to teach them how to behave appropriately will only serve to frustrate you and annoy them. With people like this, it's best to make your boundary known and then get some distance from them. Keep in mind that manipulators may try to make you feel selfish for setting limits with them, no matter how outrageous, inappropriate, or abusive their behavior is. It's not reasonable or healthy to be expected to be someone's emotional or physical punching bag. Setting boundaries isn't selfish; it's self-care.

Holding our boundaries is a primary way that we cultivate self-respect. It's impossible to simultaneously respect and erase ourselves.

Every time we give into something we don't want to, we silence our inner self. When this happens, that inner voice begins to start talking to us. It pushes back and questions why we are allowing this mistreatment. This inner voice isn't the result of low self-esteem or critical parenting, although because it's protesting or arguing with us, it may be mistaken as negative self-talk. This voice isn't your enemy; it's your friend, and it surfaces to warn you when you are unconsciously working to erase it. You can tell the difference between your internal self-critical voice and your internal authentic self-voice, by what happens when you assert your boundaries. Your internal authentic-self voice will quiet down once you start standing up for yourself—and will harbor resentment when you don't, whereas the negative self-talk that results from low self-esteem or critical parenting doesn't—if anything, the more you try to set boundaries or achieve your goals the louder and more insulting that voice becomes.

For example, let's say you go out on a date with someone who is coming on too strong. Ten minutes into the date you want to leave, but since they planned a whole evening out, you feel obligated to stay—even though your discomfort is growing. If you don't have solid boundaries, you might think any issue you have with their behavior is because you must have issues with commitment, or that you are too uptight—giving your date the benefit of the doubt because according to your internal programming, your boundaries are always wrong. The evening ends with them giving you a kiss that you didn't want—but that you gave into because you felt obligated. That night and the next morning your inner self will be upset with you and start asking why you stayed. If you aren't aware of this internal voice just yet, then it might register as icky feelings for allowing your date to talk to you like they did or to kiss you at the end of the night.

The result of situations like this are that we continually replay or rehash what happened—oftentimes wondering if their behavior was really as problematic as it felt, or if we are the ones with the issue. When we rehash or replay situations, it's usually because we've experienced a boundary violation. The more time you spend around this person, and don't make your boundaries known, the more boundary violations will occur, and the more prominent your internal voice and/or feelings of discomfort will get. If you aren't aware that your boundaries have been crossed, you will continue to misidentify any concerns you have with the behavior of others and the harsh internal voice that results, as your own unresolved issues. You may mistakenly think you are uncomfortable around this person because you have commitment issues. If you do realize that your issue with your date is their behavior, and stop seeing them, you'll find that voice becomes quiet. When you live your life according to your boundaries and standards, you'll rarely hear that voice. This voice is a lot like the guidance system in a car. If we are going the wrong way, it starts prompting us to make the next U-turn, and that voice doesn't stop until get back on track.

Standards

We all have standards, although most people have never taken the time to examine what their standards really are. If we continually find ourselves in relationships or friendships with people who mistreat us, this is a sign that it's time we raise our standards for how we *expect* to be treated. When our standards are healthy, our boundaries will inevitably become stronger—usually without much effort, as *our boundaries will always ensure that your standards are being met.*

You already have a standard in every area of your life, from the quality and quantity of food you eat, to the type of car you drive, to the job you work, to the clothes you wear, and to the people you are friends with, and the significant relationships you have. If you are curious to know what your standards are, look at the things you're currently doing.

Some examples of healthy and reasonable standards are:

- To be treated with dignity and respect by those in your inner circle.
- To have emotionally safe people in your inner circle.
- To have your inner circle and regular environment nourish you.

If we want to improve our life, we start by raising our standards. However, we can only raise our standards to the level of our self-worth and self-esteem. If we don't fully believe that we are worthy of being treated with respect, we won't expect it or insist upon it. Instead, if someone treats us poorly, we will either think their mistreatment of us is deserved or justifiable, or we will argue with them about it, trying to get them to see our worth—but we won't make it a deal breaker.

Ask yourself:

- What are my standards for those in my inner circle?
- What are my standards for those I date?

- Do I believe that I have value and bring value to others?
- Do I believe that I am worthy of having nourishing and supportive people in my life?

Deal Breakers

Having deal breakers is an important part of healthy boundaries and having a good life. If we don't have any deal breakers, this doesn't mean we are tolerant or compassionate, it means that our boundaries, standards, and self-esteem need work. It's imperative that you develop the self-awareness to know the difference between what is nourishing and what is toxic for you, so you can respond accordingly.

People with healthy deal breakers think about situations and the behavior of others in terms of *what's acceptable according to their healthy standards*. People with non-existent deal breakers interact with the world based on *how much they can handle until they are forced to walk away*. Going through life like this is not only hard; it's unnecessary. Your life will profoundly change for the better once you are able to shift your thinking from how much you *can* tolerate to what you *won't* tolerate.

If we think having deal breakers makes us inflexible or uncaring, then we will stay in situations until they become so outrageously inappropriate and unbearable that we hit our breaking point. By then our physical health is usually so negatively affected that we struggle with chronic pain, inflammation, insomnia, headaches, rashes, chronic colds, extreme fatigue, and weight gain or loss. Additionally, our emotional health is impacted, and we may now find that we are a nervous wreck, severely depressed, or anger and bitter. In extreme situations, we may have stayed to the point where this other person has become so out-of-control and dangerous that our life is on the line.

Attempting to navigate deal breakers or boundaries in the midst of manipulation is really challenging, as there is so much confusion, mental anguish, and anxiety that is occurring. Your best bet is to stop trying to untangle what all is going on and why, and instead, get clear with yourself about where your line in the sand is. What needs to happen in order for you to do something different or leave? Defining the line now can help you to see it when you get there.

As is the case with learning anything new, developing boundaries, standards, and deal breakers will take some trial and error as well as lots of practice. Radical change doesn't happen overnight. However, the good news is that you don't need radical change in order to drastically improve your life. Sometimes a few small changes in the right direction can make a profound difference.

PART 4

WINNING THE GAME

CHAPTER 26

CHANGING HOW YOU INTERACT WITH A MANIPULATOR

Once you realize you've been trying to have a relationship with someone who is playing a game, there are several ways in which you can go about changing the game so that you can restore balance into your life. The first step in this process is to decide how you are going to change the way you interact with them. There are several distancing strategies a person can use: gray rock, low contact, and no contact.

Gray Rock

If you can't go "no contact" with a manipulator because you have children with them, or you are somehow unable to get them out of your life for whatever reason, you can implement a technique called "gray rock." Gray rock is when you become as unexciting and uninteresting as, well, a gray rock. The goal is to blend into the background and become the most boring, unreactive person they've ever met so that they lose interest and move on.

They only know what you value by the level of your reaction, so beat them at their game and don't react. It helps to practice being indifferent with a trusted friend or in the mirror. Mentally rehearse the various ways they've tried to get you to respond in the past, and then practice staying emotionally neutral.

When you must engage with a manipulator, keep the conversation to surface-level topics that you would discuss with a stranger on an elevator. The goal is to avoid sharing anything emotional that is going on with you so that they don't use it against you or respond in a hurtful way. Do not talk about anything that you know will make them jealous or in any way will open the door for them to stir things up and make your life difficult. Do not talk about how great things are going for you, or any accomplishments you or your children are having, or how great your life is now that they aren't in it. Do not talk about upcoming vacations, people you are dating, recent losses or painful events you've experienced, or anything that is remotely interesting.

Don't try and get them to see how hurtful their behavior was (and is). Remember miscommunication isn't the issue. If they blame you for everything wrong in the relationship, don't fight them on this—they are never going to see things your way. Doing this takes away their ability to argue and create drama and chaos. Remain polite, professional, brief, and then be gone.

Gray rock takes practice and anticipation. You can tell you're seeing their behavior clearly when you are no longer reactive to it. Expect for their behavior to be erratic and dramatic, and it will stop catching you off guard, because *of course* they are going to act immature and irrational; it's what they do.

Low Contact

Low contact is when we have the bare minimum contact necessary with a problematic person. You will know when you have decreased contact to the right amount based on the level of frustration and anger present. If you leave their company and are rehashing conversation with yourself or a friend, then more distance is needed. Remember, you set the pace. For example, this might mean instead of following your mother's wishes that you come home for the holidays and spend two weeks with her (her setting the pace), you decide that you can only really stay for one week without losing your mind. If a large amount of mental anguish is still present, then perhaps next time three days is your limit. If that's too much, then maybe one day, or maybe a few hours—or maybe you don't go at all, and instead, call.

No Contact

No contact is when you have no contact with a dangerous or destructive person. Ideally, not only do you have no communication with them, but you aren't keeping tabs on them, checking their social media, talking to mutual friends about them, and so on. You have nothing to do with them anymore. This is for your sanity, as well as to maintain inner and outer peace in your life.

It can help to go no contact if you change your environment and get rid of any triggers that might cause you to slip into nostalgia. Rearrange furniture, put highly emotional items in a box out of sight, or donate them if you are ready, or burn them in a fire pit if you'd like. You may want to tell friends and family that you would appreciate it if they didn't keep you up-to-date on what your ex is doing, that you are trying to move on with your life. If they argue this point or tell you that you are being immature, then this is a sign that this person isn't supportive, and you may need to get some distance from them.

When you go no contact from the manipulator or other people in your life, it helps to have some sort of plan for how you will fill up the void that is left. The website meetup.com is a wonderful resource that can help you find things to do as well as to meet new people. If this appeals to you, it can be helpful to join as many meetup groups that you find even remotely interesting. This way, if you are feeling bored or lonely, you'll have a host of healthy activities available.

CHAPTER 27

CHANGING HOW YOU RESPOND

The previous chapter discussed several different ways you could interact with a problematic person. This chapter covers different ways of responding to them if you are going to keep some degree of communication open. The goal here is for you to shift out of being reactive and into being responsive. Consciously choosing how and when to respond is an important step in setting your boundaries and regaining control over restoring peace in your life.

Respond; Don't React

If you choose to, or must keep in contact with a manipulator, it can help to develop some coping strategies to help you tolerate the stress that will arise. When we cave into them or become reactive, it's generally due to a buildup of tension, being caught off guard, angry, or fearful. Here is an example of what being reactive looks like and how it can backfire:

Michelle's ex-boyfriend whom she has a restraining order against and hasn't heard from in six months, sends her a series of text messages calling her names and cussing at her, accusing her of being a selfish, manipulative whore who has ruined his life. She's knocked off guard by this, as she was hoping she'd never hear from him again, plus he was the one who was cheating, lying, and being abusive. In an attempt to set the record straight, she defends herself and calls him out on his bad behavior. Multiple texts between them ensue. This scenario ends in one of two ways: Michelle is so upset that she has a hard time regrouping, or her ex slowly moves the fight from blaming her for everything he's done to saying he loves her, and she's sucked back into this abusive relationship.

If Michelle is going to break the cycle with her ex, she's going to have to shift out of being reactive and into being responsive. I know it's absolutely infuriating to have someone who has hurt you so bad insist that they are the victim of you—especially when they've rewritten reality to do so. However, there's no point in responding to this nonsense, as doing so won't set the record straight, it will just get you back wrestling around in the mud with them--which is exactly what they want. Not responding to someone like this is still a response, and it's the most effective one, as it keeps you safe from further attacks, as well as sends the message that you aren't going to indulge their desire to get into a fight. In instances like this, not responding isn't a sign of weakness or the same thing as giving them the silent treatment. It's a sign of strength, and it's being self-protective. You don't need to engage with crazy-makers.

If you are in a situation where a response is necessary; for example, you have children or the difficult person involved is family or someone you work with, and you find yourself struggling with what to say, then it might be easier to find a reason to leave the room instead of having to come up with an immediate response. Excusing yourself to the bathroom can be a good strategy, as hopefully they won't follow. This way you can get some physical distance and regain your composure. Sometimes no response is the best response, but if you need or want to respond, after you are no longer so rattled, you can usually send them a letter or an email (or depending on your situation, have your attorney do this). By communicating in writing you are more likely to avoid saying anything impulsively, that you may regret, and it allows you to bring your best, clear-thinking, calmest self to the situation.

If you must interact with a manipulator alone, having a phrase or mantra to repeat can help keep you grounded. A mantra that I've found helpful over the years is, "I can handle this." This mantra doesn't mean that we will handle the situation perfectly, but it can give us the confidence we need, and to know that we are capable of doing the best we can. It also means that afterwards I can process and recover from the experience with the resources I have, available such as therapy, a support group, journaling, relaxation videos, etc.

Set Your Terms

You will have to teach the manipulator *through your interaction, or lack of interaction,* with them as to how you expect to be treated. Depending on the degree of manipulation and level of danger you feel you are in, sometimes it can help to establish clear boundaries and limits. If you feel setting limits might help, then tell them straight out, that you will not tolerate the silent treatment or them threatening to divorce you, fire you, etc. every time they don't get their way or when you assert yourself. If you do stand your ground like this, remember, they will view this as an attack on them. So prepare yourself for their behavior to escalate, and for the possibility that they will, for example, fire you or seek a divorce. In many situations the only way to correct this harmful imbalance which they have established, is to leave the job or the relationship. A boundary is only as strong as the consequence you back it up with. If you are fearful that standing up for yourself may make them become violent, then it's time to consider taking steps to get as far away from them as you can in the safest way possible.

When changing how you respond to them, it helps to role play potential interactions with them ahead of time. You can do this by having someone you trust play the role of them while you rehearse the different things that you could say. While you are practicing, make sure to go through some scenarios where they say or do things that would normally knock you off balance so you can practice standing your ground.

While you are practicing your response to them, make sure your vocal tone and body language match with the words you are saying. For example, if they ask you for money, and you tell them no, you want your tone to sound like you mean it. You don't want your vocal tone to rise at the end making it sound as though you are asking them a question or wanting their approval, and you don't want to sound scared or weak. When you are asserting yourself, your body language is also important. Keep your head up, shoulders back, and stand upright. Don't fidget, avoid eye contact, or hunch your shoulders. You want to send the message that you mean what you are saying and that you aren't afraid of them. The more you come across as uncertain, the more they will work to target your emotional soft spots and erode your boundaries.

You may be anxious about confrontation, but please be more anxious about the toll this dynamic is currently having on your health. If there is any chance of this dynamic being workable, it will be due to your boundaries, *not your lack of them.* If the manipulator only wants to continue this relationship if things go their way, there's no real relationship here that's worth saving.

Respond on Your Time Schedule, Not Theirs

One of the more subtle ways that manipulators control the situation is by putting their target on the spot and demanding an immediate response. They will commonly call, text, or email and push for you to get back to them right away. Don't. Even if you have the time, it's important that you break the cycle of them expecting to get what they want when they want it. Unless it is a truly urgent situation, give it some time (at least a few hours or a day) and then respond. How quickly you respond contributes to setting the pace and lets the other person know they are your top priority at the moment. You don't want to give the manipulator any sense that they have this ability and power over you.

Take time to breathe and calm down so you can think clearly. Remember, when you are asserting yourself, you are *informing* them of your boundary—*you are not asking them for permission, or for their agreement.* It may seem rude, manipulative, or as though you are playing a game if you don't get back to them right away. However, all you are doing is reclaiming your own power in the relationship, and sending a message to the manipulator that you are in ownership of your time, not them.

If your interactions with the manipulator are in person, for example, if they are a family member or co-worker, they may exert pressure through creating a tense atmosphere, not making eye contact, giving you the silent treatment, snickering, whispering, calling you names, crying, sulking, slamming doors, or being hyper-critical and fault finding in an attempt to punish you. When these methods are being used as a means to get you to respond to them, and/or do what they want, you will need to hold your ground no matter how emotionally uncomfortable you become.

Staying cool, calm, and collected when on the receiving end of anxiety-inducing behavior like this can be a challenge. If you find yourself desperate to do anything to make their behavior stop, ask yourself why this is. A lot of the tension and fear we feel comes from the threat of losing something. Are you afraid to hold your ground because they might end the relationship, get you fired, or cause you to lose clients or friends? Whatever answer you come up with, ask yourself how you would handle things if that were to happen, and come up with a plan to address the worst-case scenario. If you fear losing friends, maybe it's time to start meeting some new people now. If you fear your spouse leaving you, then maybe it would help to seek out a support group, open up a bank account at a different bank in your name only, and spend time cultivating existing or new friendships so you have support if this were to happen. If you fear them firing you, then maybe it's time to put together a resume or to start looking for a new job. Identifying the deeper fear and how you will handle it will empower you to interact with them from a place of strength, not a place of fear.

Interacting with a manipulative adult is a lot like interacting with a manipulative child. If you say no ten times but then cave in on the eleventh, you have just lost all the ground you had previously gained, and then some. The next time you say no, or set a boundary, they realize that you can be worn down with time and pressure, and in any future interactions with them, it will be more difficult to hold your ground, but you will have to if things are going to change.

Repeat What You've Said

Once you've asserted yourself, it's important to stand your ground and repeat *only* what you told them originally. Do not start discussing, debating, or defending your actions. A great way to remember to avoid doing this is with the acronym "JADE," which stands for "Justify," "Argue," "Defend," or "Explain." If you do start to JADE, they are dragging you off course and into the mud so that they can wrestle around with you. For most manipulators, if they can just get their target into the mud, they consider this a win. You've already said what you need to say. There's no need to keep repeating or arguing the point, and this isn't the time to discuss other issues. You are informing them how the issue at hand is going to happen according to your boundaries.

For example, your ex calls with a question about the time your child's piano recital starts. You give them the time, and then they proceed to become rude, attacking, and demanding, wanting to know if you are going to bring a date, or complaining about how expensive the lessons are and how this is the last month they will be paying for them and so on. Don't get pulled into the mud by defending yourself or how important these piano lessons are to your child, or getting upset that they are going to go back on their word to split the cost of the lessons with you. Take a deep breath, and stay as nonreactive as possible. Reiterate the time of the piano recital and where it's going to be and then end the conversation.

Disarm the Manipulation

One way to disarm manipulation is to address their behavior directly. However, I must warn you that doing so most likely won't go over well, and can quickly escalate. This tactic is only to be used with the manipulators out there who are on the annoying or frustrating end of the spectrum, and never with someone violent or that you fear might become violent.

For example, say they give you the silent treatment after you've disagreed with them or asserted yourself. You could tell them that you understand they are upset, but that giving you the silent treatment is not okay with you. You could let them know that if they need time to cool down that's fine, but to give you a day when they plan on reopening communication. Plan for them to shift the topic back to everything you do that they don't appreciate. Do not engage in defending yourself or getting into an argument. Stick to the topic at hand. So if they start saying something such as, "I don't care that you don't like the silent treatment. I don't like the way you dress." You could counter that with something like, "Well, you have every right to not like how I dress, but for now, I'd like to stay on the topic of the silent treatment and how I'd like for us to communicate in a more effective way." (By letting someone know that they have the right to feel the way they do doesn't mean you are saying that you agree with them. It's simply acknowledging their feelings.)

These strategies take time and practice, but they are doable. In time, you will find yourself interacting with others in a whole new and empowered way, and you will find it hard to believe there was ever a time you did anything different.

CHAPTER 28

DEVELOPING YOUR STRATEGIES

You have more insight than you may realize when it comes to developing strategies to interact with the manipulator in your life.

What have you tried in the past to prevent yourself from not getting sucked in, flustered, or enraged by their behavior? Have you tried asserting yourself and setting boundaries with them before? Examine what has and hasn't worked. The answers to these questions are the starting point for developing your new plan. The more clarity you have for what does and doesn't work, the more you can anticipate their moves and your counter moves.

The best predictor of a manipulator's future behavior is their past behavior. If they have a history of pushing your buttons in a certain way, develop a plan to anticipate that they will continue to push your buttons in a similar way in the future. However, this does not mean that their future behavior won't be worse than their past behavior. It often is.

Once you can start to anticipate what they are doing to try and knock you off balance, it won't come as such a shock. If anything, if they *don't* try and knock you off balance, then this is the time to be shocked. Even if a manipulator starts acting in a caring, concerned, or compassionate way, you would be wise to keep your guard up, as this good behavior isn't the same thing as change, and is usually only another level to their game. Opening up to a manipulator in any way, shape, or form and letting your guard down can get you sucked right back in. Keep your emotional shields up, and keep contact to a minimum if you must have any contact at all. It can be hard to let go of the fantasy of the relationship you could have—especially when they are on their best behavior, or if things have seemed to turn a corner, *but remember there's a difference between a person truly changing and them just acting the part.*

Now that you know the game you are playing, the players in the game, who is on your team, you are going to need some strategies as to how to actually win this game.

Strategy #1: Stop seeking clarity from the person with whom you feel perpetually confused around.

Confusion is always the first sign of a problem, no matter how fleeting that confusion may be. Confusion is a powerful sign that we tend not to give enough credit when we do experience it. If someone has confusing behavior that feels either unsettling or too good to be true, it's a good idea to get some physical and emotional distance from them so you can think more clearly about how to proceed. One way to do this is to ask yourself if this is a situation you would want a good friend or your child in. If you would be concerned if a loved one is in this situation, then ask yourself why you think this situation is okay for you.

The number one mistake that targets make is that when they feel confused by the manipulator's behavior they ask the manipulator for clarity. If the manipulator is trying to keep you roped into their game, they won't give you clarity; they will only add more confusion by either telling you what you want to hear or giving you excuses. This will only serve to get you further into their web.

To stop seeking clarity from a manipulator can feel counter-intuitive for a person who is seeking a solution and thinks that more communication will help. After all, communication should give way to clarity. And this is the case as long as you are dealing with a person who has a team-oriented reality. If you find yourself in a situation where any additional communication on your part only seems to make things worse or adds additional confusion, there is something wrong—especially if you don't have this issue with other people in your life.

Strategy #2: Anticipate nostalgia, minimization, and well-intended bad advice.

The ending of any relationship can be difficult, no matter how toxic the dynamic is, or how angry you are with them. If the manipulative person in your life is a parent or a partner, it can be difficult to give up the fantasy of the relationship you wanted to have with them. The pull of this fantasy can be hard to resist, and it's the main reason why people continue to go back.

In order to prevent this pull, it can help to anticipate "craving" the fantasy and for nostalgia to kick in, so that you can prepare yourself if and when this happens. One way to do this is to write out all of the reasons this relationship isn't good for you. If you have screenshots of terrible things they've said, keep those. If and when you are tempted to reopen contact with them, read your list and look at your screenshots. The goal here is to remind yourself of the pain that comes with having them in your life. Don't slip into minimizing their behavior, or thinking that maybe you could be friends or casual acquaintances with them—especially when their track record is that they have caused you a lot of pain and shown no lasting signs of change. Holding on to hope in a dynamic like this isn't being optimistic; it's being in denial.

Strategy #3: Understand that there is always an angle.

Manipulators seek to get their way at the expense of others, while malignant manipulators seek to get their way at the *destruction* of others. It's how they interact with the world, and go about getting their needs (and hidden agendas) met. Everything is a game to them, and every move they make has a purpose—even if their "move" seems harmless or even considerate.

For example, your ex offers to take you and your children to lunch so they can apologize for their "hurtful" and insensitive (abusive) behavior. They bring small gifts for the children, apologize to you, and the rest of the lunch goes smoothly—ideally even. You didn't know they were capable of such appropriate conversation or thoughtfulness. They even go so far as to video the lunch, with everyone smiling and laughing. You think this is a little odd, but chalk their behavior up to them being excited to see the kids. Lunch ends with them promising to call that night to say goodnight to the kids. You leave thinking that maybe they finally understand how hurtful their behavior has been and hopeful that they will be a more involved parent from here on out. But that night they don't call, and you have two children to console. You fire off several angry texts to your ex about what a jerk they are and that you are tired of them being such an awful parent and that your kids deserve better.

Several days later you find out that they've posted the video of your lunch visit on social media along with some screenshots of the angry texts you'd later sent—painting the picture that they want to be a doting and involved father, but because of your abusive and controlling behavior, you won't let them. Your jaw drops and you sit frozen in stunned disbelief. Once the shock wears off, you start to realize just how damaging and manipulative their post really is. Mutual friends, family, former coworkers, and people at your church all begin commenting on it, showing support for your ex. You are mortified as you start to realize lunch and a promise to call the kids was all a ploy to make you look bad. You call your best friend upset and in a panic, trying to explain that you were set up. Realizing how paranoid and emotionally unhinged you sound, you end the conversation unsure of what to do or how to do damage control.

The example above isn't extreme, and unfortunately, some version of this set up is common with manipulators. The lesson to learn here is to treat each and every interaction with them as if you'd have to defend your actions to a judge. You want to stay in control and by staying ahead of their games, as much as possible, in order to avoid being in a one-down position and having to scramble and to do damage control. The only way to stay in control is to keep your guard up and assume that everything they do has some sort of angle. If their previous behavior has shown that they are manipulative, do not let a few seemingly considerate acts paint a new picture of them. This isn't you being paranoid; this is you being protective. As the saying goes, you aren't being paranoid if they really are out to get you.

Strategy #4: Getting a witness to your reality.

Document every communication possible in order to create a paper trail. And view your every response as though you'd have to explain yourself to a judge. Additionally, you would be wise to assume that they are doing the same thing, *so be mindful of what you say and how you say it.* Even if no legal actions are even taken, keeping a written trail of all the crazy-making can help to validate your experience.

CHAPTER 29

PRACTICING YOUR STRATEGIES

By this point in the book, you are seeing your behavior and the behavior of others in a whole new way. While the thought of changing how you interact with the manipulator may feel overwhelming, with practice and time, the skills you are learning will become second nature, and there will come a day when you won't believe you ever interacted with people differently.

So here are some ways to set yourself up for success:

- Prepare and practice to be knocked off balance. One of the biggest shifts that we can make in disabling manipulative behavior is to expect for them do and say things to knock you off balance, and to have a pre-planned response what you will say or do ahead of time.

- Prepare and practice how you can keep your distance from them. If you have down time around them and want to avoid conversation, you could, for example, plan to stay busy returning emails, texting a friend, or using some headphones to listen to music.

- <u>Prepare and practice some responses ahead of time.</u> Mentally rehearse what you could say in order to excuse yourself from the situation, or as a response to being backed into a corner. For example, if you know going to your parents' house for the holidays will result in them shaming or ridiculing you, either limit your time there or make alternate plans, if possible. You'll know the right level of distance you need is based on how calm or agitated you feel. The more agitated you are, the more your plan needs some revision.

- <u>Prepare to need support.</u> Lining up some support before and ideally after you know you will encounter a problematic person or a difficult event (such a court date, birthday party, holiday, etc.) can help to relieve some of your stress. For example, you could speak to a good friend or therapist before and/or after the anxiety-inducing experience to help you prepare for it as well as to decompress from it. However, while getting support can be tremendously helpful, it's not a substitute for taking corrective action where you can—it's only relieving the stress you have in the moment. For example, it's common for targets to struggle with shifting out of hoping and coping and to start being assertive and setting boundaries (assuming that doing so is safe). What tends to happen is they get into therapy or a support group and vent for months or years on end thinking that this is being productive, without actually doing anything different. For what it's worth, I did this for decades before I realized if I wanted to restore peace in my life, I was going to have to set limits with other people.

CONCLUSION

If you are like most people (myself included), who are drawn to this topic, your initial goal was to better understand a specific problematic person in your life. What you may not have anticipated was that understanding manipulative behavior leads to a series of rabbit holes to explore, each one leading to more clarity and more unanswered questions. This might leave you feeling disoriented and confused, much like Alice in Wonderland, with your understanding of the world flipped upside down with each new rabbit hole. Feeling this way is normal and is all part of the process of massive personal growth. With time and observation, I've come to realize that there are four big rabbit holes of awareness that are necessary to see the behavior of others and ourselves more clearly. However, the challenge is that each of these rabbit holes can contribute to a tremendous amount of self-doubt and anxiety and cause a person to stop moving forward or to run back to what they know.

At this point in the book, you are, at a minimum, in the process of going down the first rabbit hole.

Understanding the First Rabbit Hole

The first rabbit hole is understanding that many of the messages we've been given about love, friendship, commitment, how to solve problems, and how to spot problematic people are incomplete at best, and incorrect at worst. This can be terrifying, and for those who were deeply wounded by a pathological person, this can lead to a burning, almost obsessive, desire to understand personality disorders (especially narcissistic, antisocial, and borderline personality disorder). This search often leads to many hours comparing and contrasting information trying to figure out exactly what kind of personality disorder the problematic person in their might have, or if this person is "just" a normal crazy-maker with relationship-destroying behavior who is eroding your boundaries. The main focus people in this phase tend to have is with trying to discern the difference between normal and deeply problematic behavior. It's around this point that they get caught up in well-intended bad advice and frequently second guess what they are considering problematic as they are still holding onto the fears of missing out on a good person and being too uncompromising with the boundaries and standards they are developing.

Understanding that there are people in this world who are so profoundly destructive is really confusing, and it can feel that the only way we can keep ourselves safe is by understanding what we are up against. However, it's important to realize that this problematic person in your life is more than likely not the first and they won't be the last. It's vital that you are able to extend your understanding of all of the information—how you perceive behavior in general—and not limit your understanding to the problematic person in your life. The challenge with this is that you start to see problematic behavior everywhere—but you are the only one who sees it. Other people in your life are quick to deny, minimize, or excuse it, and this might make you question whether you are being hyper-vigilant or if what you are seeing is, in fact, a problem. The odds are that what you are seeing is a problem and you aren't making a big deal out of nothing or being hyper-vigilant. Unfortunately, we live in a dysfunctional society and nothing in this book is common knowledge—or taught, at least not to the extent it needs to.

The Biggest Challenges with the First Rabbit Hole:

- **To begin to find your voice again.** It might help to start small and get in tune with your wants, needs, and opinions—even if you don't act on them, don't think you have any, or they aren't that strong. For example, your friend asks you where you want to go to lunch, and you have no preference. Even if you don't care if you have Chinese food or pizza, the goal here is to make a decision and to assert yourself; so pick one. You could also go window shopping or go through your closet and ask yourself what you do and don't like and why. And yes, little decisions and opinions like this do make a difference—especially if you make it a point to make them on a regular basis. You will be surprised as to the level of self-awareness this simple exercise will bring you in the next six or so months.

- **To begin to turn inward for answers instead of asking others—especially if you are traumatized or have PTSD.** Practice getting clear on what you do think and why, even if you doubt your answers. At a minimum, come up with your own opinion and supporting reasons why before you seek validation from someone else. You may also want to journal about this so that you can go back with the benefit of hindsight and see how these different decisions played out and why, and examine how close they were to your perception of events.

- **To get in tune with when you are being mistreated.** Now that you know a lot more about manipulation and abuse, as well as "problematic" behavior in general, you will start to become aware of when you and others are being treated with disdain, contempt, or hostility. You may start seeing this behavior a lot more frequently and wonder if you are being hyper-vigilant. Odds are you aren't, because there is no shortage of this kind of behavior out there, and it can be really unsettling when you start to see it for what it is.

- **To understand learning about manipulation and the various types of manipulative people is only the beginning.** If there is one point that trips people up and gets them stuck, it's this one. Learning about manipulation techniques, abuse, narcissists, sociopaths, and other types of manipulators is extremely helpful and can go a long way to keep you safe; however, this is just the tip of the iceberg. The magic happens when we start to examine the various ways we were socialized in not protecting ourselves in the first place and are able to begin correcting this deficit by learning what it means to value ourselves.

- **To realize that your healing doesn't end here.** Healing from manipulation and the emotional devastation that comes with this doesn't mean going back to the way you were, and it doesn't mean no longer feeling suicidal or being able to cope with the pain. It means understanding the world and yourself in a new and empowering way, creating a new normal for yourself, and working through your feelings along the way.

Understanding the Second Rabbit Hole

The second rabbit hole people go down is when they realize whatever relationship brought them to a book like this isn't the first problematic relationship they've had in their life. The one that brought them here might have been the most painful or the most over-the-top bizarre thing you've ever experienced, but odds are it wasn't the only one. This realization takes most people years to have, and I hope that by my pointing it out, you can begin connecting the dots sooner rather than later. It's worth taking the time to list the various problematic dynamics you've had in your life and to explore what these relationships had in common.

The Biggest Challenges with the Second Rabbit Hole:

- **To make the connections between these different relationships.** Every problematic dynamic in your past is most likely different. Some might have been crazy-making, and some might have been scary or even dangerous. Some might have been with "friends," family members, significant others, coworkers, neighbors, or people at your church or place of worship.

- **To make the correct connections between these different relationships.** It's easy to link an incorrect cause and effect and to think that the people that caused you pain did so because they were men, or had a certain astrological sign, or some other defining feature. It is essential to realize that problematic behavior is the problem—all these other factors are not the issue.

- **To continue to validate yourself.** As you start connecting the dots, you will most likely come across other people who will tell you that you are hyper-vigilant and making a big deal out of nothing. The more you understand covert and overt forms of manipulation and abuse, the easier it will be for you to understand and validate your experience.

- **To not try to force others into seeing problematic behavior for what it is.** Most people are in deep denial and don't want to face the facts that someone is abusive or manipulative, especially if that person is a family member.

- **To move from knowing when you are being mistreated, to getting in tune with what is comfortable and uncomfortable for you.** Once you start to get in tune with what it feels like when you are being mistreated, the next step is to get in tune with what uncomfortable situations or behavior feels like when it first starts. The next step in this process is to begin navigating boundaries in situations like these—regardless of what anyone else thinks of the situation or what you should do.

Understanding the Third Rabbit Hole

The third rabbit hole involves an even further expansion of awareness. Now you are starting to see problematic behavior in society. You begin to see the problematic messages that are circulated and seen as either harmless or as truth. Certain themes in movies (especially romantic comedies), music lyrics, and TV shows may leave you with feelings of disgust and concern, that stalking, abuse, and control are mistaken as romantic. (I have some videos on my website that address this in more detail if you are interested:

www.thriveafterabuse.com/movies).

You may find certain messages or advice from your spiritual leader, counselor, or best friend lacking the context of healthy boundaries. You start to become more aware of the patterns you were in before and are better able to slow them down and do something more balanced and empowering for everyone involved. Your inner circles start to shift and you begin to seek out people who have a healthier understanding of boundaries—both of yours and of their own, to where dignity and respect are freely given and not something you need to fight or beg for. Around this time, you find it difficult and uncomfortable to be around emotionally immature and manipulative people and the various crazy-making conversations that result. Additionally, outside of feeling frustrated, you may find that you are starting to notice physical symptoms that arise when you are around toxic behavior and situations—as though you literally feel the toxicity and it's making you sick. You might notice headaches, fatigue, an upset stomach, or your skin might start breaking out. Because your discomfort continues to grow, setting boundaries and getting the distance you need become significantly easier.

The Biggest Challenges with the Third Rabbit Hole:

- **Feeling like you don't belong.** You start seeing concerning behavior more frequently, and yet, other people don't seem to notice. This can make you feel like an outsider when you are around other people who have no issue being around certain family members or problematic people.

- **Self-doubt.** Even though you are getting better at validating yourself, you may still struggle with wondering if your standards and boundaries are too high—especially if you are feeling lonely. At this stage, you are relating to people in a very different way, and you may find that even if you do try and lower your standards, doing so is painful, because you are craving the company of empowering, nourishing people who are in tune with who they are.

- **Reshuffling your inner circle.** You may find that you are wanting or needing to distance yourself from quite a few people. There may come a point where you realize that while your circle is healthier, it's a lot smaller than you'd like it to be. A great way to meet new people is with the website meetup.com, and the best thing is that you can meet people based on certain interests such as personal growth or whatever hobbies may interest you.

Understanding the Fourth Rabbit Hole

The fourth rabbit hole is seeing your own problematic thoughts and behavior. Perhaps this was behavior that you developed as a way to cope around dysfunctional people, or maybe it was the result of dysfunctional messages about who you are and who you should be. This awareness comes into focus a little at a time, and if we are introspective and dedicated to personal growth, is something that will be a life-long process. This doesn't mean that we are deeply flawed and must sit on the bench of life and wait until we are fully healed and self-aware before we date, cultivate friendships, or even simply have fun. It simply means that we, like all of the other people out there who are interested in self-development, are striving towards self-actualization—and that this is a journey. The best thing about the fourth rabbit hole is that you will start to come across other fellow travelers who are like-minded—people that you always hoped existed but never knew where to find them.

The Biggest Challenge with the Fourth Rabbit Hole:

Being open to exploring dysfunctional messages you've unknowingly received. This is the biggest hurdle for people—myself included, in part because we don't know what dysfunctional messages we've received because we view them as truth, and in part it can feel like victim blaming to even insinuate that our social programming could have played a part in us being hurt. This is especially the case if our world view has never caused us harm before, or for many "helpers" of the world, being kind, compassionate, forgiving, and tolerant can seem virtuous—and nowhere near the zip code of problematic. For many of us, these traits are taken to an extreme and consequently imbalanced, causing us harm in ways we most likely aren't consciously aware of. When this is the case, these damaging relationships can seem like a fluke, and that had we known about these kinds of people we wouldn't have gotten tangled up with them. This is only half correct. If these traits remain imbalanced and our vulnerabilities remain unexplored, we will continue to run the risk of getting caught up with problematic people.

Additionally, it takes most people years before they've been able to process enough of the hurt and anger to even be open to the idea of exploring their vulnerabilities and any problematic messages they may have about love, friendship, commitment, boundaries, and forgiveness—if they ever get to that point. It's important to realize that this imbalance isn't just with you; society is dysfunctional and the messages we are all taught lack the context of what it means to be self-protective. Instead, most people are taught the opposite: that being a good person means to sink ourselves to save others.

Many people get consumed by this pain and as a result feel broken and become bitter and jaded. If this describes where you currently are, please know that this is a normal stage in healing and that you don't have to get stuck here. It can help to view yourself as badly bruised and forever changed, but the bruises can heal and the ways you've been changed don't have to all be for the worst. With time, many survivors are able to squeeze out dozens of lessons from these experiences and not only rebuild a better life for themselves despite what happened, but rebuild a better life *because* of what happened.

In fact, the only people I've come across who fully have the awareness needed to effectively see manipulation for what it is, disable it when it occurs, and equate loving themselves with being self-protective are those who have had their lives blown apart by problematic people and who have consequently been able to go down each of these four rabbit holes in this section. The reason is that we often need total destruction in order to not only rebuild, but to *consciously* rebuild, examining every piece to make sure it's a good fit. So please don't make the mistake of looking around at others who haven't had the world destroyed and think that everyone else has it all figured out or is healthy or well-adjusted. I've encountered many mental health clinicians and "relationship experts" who have this same dysfunctional programming and don't realize it. You can tell where someone's world view is based upon how they speak about the various topics I mentioned before (relationships, love, commitment, friendship, boundaries, etc.) A person who has dysfunctional messages that are running their behavior has unhealthy understanding of some or all of these things. In my book *Out of the Fog,* I cover several dozen frequently-confused concepts that occur when a healthy context is missing, such as:

- A person being friendly and a person being a friend
- A predator and a parent
- A manipulationship and a relationship

- Trauma bonds and healthy bonds
- Tolerating abuse and a person not being perfect
- Sincerity and intensity
- Selfishness and self-love
- Deal breakers and workable behavior
- A person acting the part and them actually changing

In order for our lives to work, balance must be restored and continually tended to. The only way this is possible is to know how to be self-protective and value our time, energy, emotions, body, and environment around us as well as to be able to discern the difference between healthy messages and dysfunctional ones. Many of these dysfunctional messages and their functional counterpart have been addressed in this book. They include:

- Understanding the two different mindsets (Chapter 7).
- Understanding your vulnerabilities (Chapter 24).
- Understanding healthy boundaries, standards, deal breakers (Chapter 26).
- Understanding common personality traits that are exploited (Chapter 25).
- Understanding what type of self-esteem you have (Chapter 25).
- Understanding the problem with needing external validation (Chapter 25).
- Understanding what type of locus of control you have (Chapter 25).

- Understanding the stages of change--and where another person is within these stages, where your expectations for them are, and where your own behavior is in response to them (Chapters 17 and 18).

The journey through healing isn't something that you have to go on alone. Tens of thousands of people across the world are in our support groups as I type this. We were once afraid, overwhelmed, lonely, resentful, and felt broken beyond repair. Many thought that they would never smile or feel joy again. Through the validation, understanding, knowledge, and support of others who have been through this, we've been able to restore peace and balance to our lives. So please come and join us at www.thriveafterabuse.com!

About the Author

Dana Morningstar is an abuse educator, focusing on awareness and prevention, as well as recovery, healing, and self-esteem. She seeks to empower those who have been abused to reclaim their power, boundaries, confidence, and identity. In addition to being an author, she has a blog, podcast, runs a large support group, and hosts a three-hour live stream every Wednesday night on her YouTube channel, "Thrive After Abuse." In her free time, she enjoys relaxing on Lake Michigan, practicing aerial yoga, reading, and gardening.

Printed in Great Britain
by Amazon